⌐RY

JANE GRIFFITHS

ANOTHER COUNTRY

NEW & SELECTED POEMS

BLOODAXE BOOKS

Copyright © Jane Griffiths 2000, 2005, 2008

ISBN: 978 1 85224 794 2

First published 2008 by
Bloodaxe Books Ltd,
Highgreen,
Tarset,
Northumberland NE48 1RP.

www.bloodaxebooks.com
For further information about Bloodaxe titles
please visit our website or write to
the above address for a catalogue.

Bloodaxe Books Ltd acknowledges
the financial assistance of
Arts Council England,
North East.

London Borough
of Lambeth

LM 1171633 9	
Askews	12-Sep-2008
821.914 GRI	£9.95

Cover design: Neil Astley & Pamela Robertson-Pearce.

Printed in Great Britain by
Bell & Bain Limited, Glasgow, Scotland.

For Nigel, after all

ACKNOWLEDGEMENTS

This book includes poems from two previous collections published by Bloodaxe Books, *A Grip on Thin Air* (2000) and *Icarus on Earth* (2005), together with a new collection, *Eclogue Over Merlin Street* (2008).

Acknowledgements are due to the editors of the following publications in which some of the previously uncollected poems first appeared: *Branch-Lines: Edward Thomas and Contemporary Poetry*, ed. Guy Cuthbertson & Lucy Newlyn (Enitharmon Press, 2007), *Chatter of Choughs*, ed. Lucy Newlyn (The Hypatia Trust, 2005), *Edinburgh Review*, *Oxford Poetry*, *Signals Magazine* and *The Times Literary Supplement*. I should also like to thank Polly Clark and Esther Morgan for some tremendously helpful and enjoyable discussions of early drafts of several of these poems.

CONTENTS

FROM **A GRIP ON THIN AIR** (2000)

Eclogue Over Merlin Street

(2008)

Blue

is for the improbable
hightail of a swallow against the opal
eyepatch of morning,
the sky-shard of an egg, nested.
The light at 4 A.M. finetuning.

For the fourposter of the house sprung
from its floorplan and a twist
of pencil shavings. For the impermeable
iris rim of the horizon, the raw
note of rooks or a pigeon swell-throated

and sticking over, over on the stairwell
of the scales. For a broken catch,
the shed at the garden's edge
lavender in a heathaze of bees.
For the eye of a needle or thinking

the new house from the old just as
a dog fox, covert and enormous,
threads through the grass and exits,
leaving the breakthrough of the fence,
the child's swing swinging: jangled, electric.

White Song

Like bread, like new-risen linen fresh against
the tight translucent sheet of sky. Like the crest

of toothpaste spilling from its cup, the clean
sweep of a brushful of paint or revelation

between two rungs of a ladder. Like thought
without words, something not yet begun.

Like the sudden outcome in algebra, space
looped in an ascender, noises off, a mill race.

Like words without tongue. Like a day's
unplanned truancy, the fretwork of a cage,

an open door. The blur of a 70s TV screen,
the electric undertow in a cat's long fur

or Jack's drainpipes and Meg's stilettos.
Like the tiger's changed stripes, a tongue's twist

of vanilla ice cream, air wind-whisked in
wake of a mouse, the Atlantic riding

over whole phone conversations. Like a backdrop,
a bell-jar, a pure invention, this is the house:

Stock

Across the valley birds go about their turnovers:
single sparrows and crows, pigeons tumbling
like outsize bullet points into the birch

and a quick black calligraphy of starlings
passing in knife-edge italic against the cloud.
Two gardens down an old man weights his henhouse

roof with row upon row of last year's apples.
Hounds call elliptically over the hill.
The fields are barred with a feathering of snow.

In the foreground there's a tree or three or four
in a corkscrew twist, just a few loose leaves
of what could be honeysuckle rotating lightly

through sixty degrees and back against long lines
of fences and cross-hatched plots, sheds, and the shell
of a caravan next door but one. It's so simple

you could live here: with the ancient, unnameable
tree, the rows of apples, and birds turning over and over
the cadmium blue stable you'd forgotten you own.

Homing

I

The sentence, of course, is for a year
and a day. The house dormant, month
after month sleepwalking across the stone.
The sharp impressions of May come

round again: horse chestnuts fleshing out,
the willow feathering.
                              Up front, a pigeon
that freights the pinheads of honeysuckle
and the hills each day a little closer.

There are rumours of roads, yes: root
and branch systems, long green tunnels
where one thing leads to another and slips
of cow parsley pointedly repeat.

We make shift with furniture, exchange views.
Lilac sends up flares over the outhouse roof
where the road converges with the ridge of the hill
like a sentence springing naturally from the premises.

II

Some nights, driving back, the stars stand out
from all the accretions about them: the time-
lag flashing the latest news from 4 May 1542

BC or thereabouts, and how this spelled our future
all those light years ago.
                              And some nights, too,
houses are a trick of the dark behind

the endless upright repeats of pine and conifer
curbing the road. Like a solidity, like the idea
of being somewhere. Like arriving to find

the place where you left it: the three storeys
in the thick of the hill, the heavy ring
to the gatelatch, and the key turning slowly

as a sleeper waking from her recurrent dream.

And then there was the night the conservatory
roof blew off, just a segment of it skewed

in corrugated geometry in the flowerbed.
Overhead the sky startled in sheer proximity.
The stars plotted their usual courses.

III

Some days, driving back, these are the things
you remember: the silhouette of leaves shifting

darkly behind the leaves, the forest green
and double-edged. And hard to articulate, being

in it, as you always are, where there are always
the trees. In the beginning was the house

behind the trees. In the beginning
was a branch, a bifurcation.

In the beginning was the sentence with a turn
sudden as the piebald horse where you turn

to go over the bridge by the railway by
the sign advertising *baths enamelled, pine*

stripped, marital problems solved: where
the horse grazes each summer, in early summer:

regular as print, or the leaves turning.

Today you arrived at it unexpectedly, turning

out on the road in a small vehicle among
the straight and narrow trunks, the roughage

of firs: the things you think through.
And it all came back to you: May and the cow

parsley repeating its shaky constellations
as it was in the beginning, the stone

waxing and waning as the sun inches across,
and how it is lost to you, and continuous.

The Man Who Mapped the World One-to-One

He started small. On his bedroom floor
a crayoned X marked the spot, another
was off somewhere behind the water tower.

Three Cs stood for a mermaid, a visible
twist of wind, to the north, for dragons.
The scale was morse, long-short-long,

and all his arrows were feathered:
his compass points flew, as the crow flies,
circuitously. Then he grew.

He thought land was for combing; he bought
a pedometer, tracked the golden miles with
each turn of the wheel hissing *est*, *est*, *est*.

He was less clear about the cutting down
to size: the cutting out of here a postbox,
there a bay tree or the bay horse

with a mulch of grass and thirty-two
grains of sand ringed in the halo of light
that was its shoe. He dreamed of crawling

up the country, smoothing it, inch by inch
to its own perfect footprint: *as is, as is.*
He started from home, charted the constituent

parts of each stone, the triple joints of a twig:
he couldn't match them. He compromised, drew
a stick insect. A crow came to nest in it.

And when he unclipped the sheets from the line
and laid them flat in the garden, it rained.
The leaves turned. He made a memorandum.

A drop spilled from the broken gutter, spun
the world three times over, and split.
The crow passed, inverted. He kept his ear

to the ground. Spread-eagled, he heard grass
edging the sheets, pushing through them
and round him, marking his place.

A Room of One's Own

Evenings, the mind gets to work behind closed doors,
turns up the light on *Truth and Allegory*
in Stephen Hawes or *Women Poets Anthologised.*

The window frames shady morphologies of hazel,
quince, and conifer, conifer, all their angles
poised and shifting with something like the noise

a thought makes, settling in. And between them
a great glass globe looped with pendant clauses
of brilliants, vines. And above them, the moon.

The open book on the desk tells how a djinn
comes spinning out of the green of a night
light to grant three golden wishes, spherical

as fruit, and how there are no other choices.
That the towers of grammar and rhetoric hold
the key, that the lady is a figure in the music

the knight hears fluted, now and then, from a clearing.
That repetition is sevenfold, like dragons, and why:
By worde the worlde was made orygynally.

The desk in the wood is mahogany, leather and solid
gilt among the blind tooling of the leaves. A small
enamelled horse rolls a cartload of stars along it

and through the trees' crossed purposes, their dark
fluting on the pages repeating over and over how
there is nothing new under – how there is nothing –

And the stop, the catch in the breath, when the lady enters the room.

Train Time

(after a wood-engraving by Anne Hayward)

Preparing for the journey she sets out
her tools against the dark
wood, burnished and midnight blue

and with a deep breath the train
eases from beneath the coving:
a fine white incision and shavings

flecked from the graver like sparks
from the wheels or high notes
in the song of the undercarriage

and the rails as it builds
like light gathering in the folds
of hedgerows massive as boulders

and the soft pleat of all the material
world around her.
                              Drawing on
the sun grows hard-pressed as glass

against the leaves, fields crossed
hatch shadows before the sudden
deep of an embankment, grasses

bleeding through the fingers, hair
running to seed. And not knowing
where to make an end of it.

Across the aisle, a man with gold
ore veining his shirt sleeves.
The sun sheared through the viaduct.

The stippling of solid air.
That girl in the corner looking
as if she might change here.

Metamorphosis

First, the quickening of the bare forked
extremities: multiple digits flexing like leaves.

The most distant outrunners underground growing
sensible, fretting the weight of the earth

with such a fine toehold it's like feeling the grass
edge upward the length of centuries: this slow

branching out from the tight contracted kernel
of the self, relearning attachments

and the sheer sensation of passing through
the air: all the wooden cages let slip

in a harsh clatter of rooks startled skywards
as the boughs drop from newly-fledged

joints to hang with an almost human curvature,
the pinions of the trunk spring away

and the spine discovers the possibilities
of rotation. Fleshing out their untouchable

dead wood, lesser branches turn muscular,
tendentiously grasp straws from the loose-

leaved hair. An awkward graft at shoulder
height redefines itself as the jut of a hipbone.

Last, the pulse of lungs and heart beats
return return return: one by one her feet

leave the earth and the woman steps clean
out of the wood, shaking free her skirt

and standing with a kind of gravity in
the open in her own skin as in a nutshell.

Accidental

(for Mary)

Supposing there'd been trains, we'd have made the view –
the smooth red ball snickering across the grass, one of us
stooping, thumbs loosely caged on the mallet, and its head
levered slowly upward to the top of its arc.

The portico and dome hovering like an idea of permanence
someone had just sketched in –
                                                    and then the swing
of the shaft skimming the top of its shadow, the jagged crack
of impact and the black ball whispering down the path of the red,

touching and twinned with it –
                                                but this isn't how it happened.
The grounds were private and there were no witnesses to a game
that started late and ran on till the hoops in the sun stretched
to railway arches, enormous articulated giants lagged beside us,

mallets the size of swinging boats at a fair.
                                                            And on, as the sun
set and we flagged the hoops by voice – *aim left a bit – no,
over here* – and as the game grew devious it was impossible
to tell the moment when the dome blacked out and the hoops

became moonshine and we realised that *this was the day
we played croquet in the dark* because there was just the click-
click-click of the invisible balls spinning forward and a voice
in the distance crying *that was hopeless, you missed by miles.*

Angles on Jacob's Ladder

It is old and there are ways of getting round it.

From the new causeway it is matchstick:
an arrangement of fine white rules against
the cliff. We reach the sea in a minute flat,

hardly think of our fathers and uncles
in shorts, holding the handrail, their mothers
in shady hats, following with the picnic.

Still, it is a marker. Looking back at low tide
a single white streak signals *too far* from the tiny
adults huddled round their flasks and garibaldi.

By night, divers swarm down it in dark clusters,
peel off, launch themselves from the railing:
invisible, and out, out, out. The sea opens and shuts.

The ladder stands above it all like a searchlight.
It is strictly abstract, uncompromising:
there are three hundred and sixty-nine steps

(there are eighty-one). The alternate white treads,
measured absences mark progress in a calculation
of faith: it is plumb, it is true as spirit levels,

and it is knots, silver-sanded grain and jagged
splinters in the quick of the thumb. Rusted
bolts, a green and fronded stain, a hanging

question to be solved by climbing, foot
by foot to the sudden thicket of pansies, the sand-
stone arch and fuchsias trumpeting crimson.

The solid thrum of bees louder than the sea.

But there are ways of getting round it. Along-
side, a child knuckles up the cliff face, cheek

to rock and sensing the gravity of the space below
her: what the divers saw, but more slowly. The flats
of the beach huts, the curve to the steps, the railing,

the weight of the world swinging over and over.

Territorial

When the freeze came, we didn't think it strange.
It was the first winter in the new house, in
the new language. There were no known laws.

The small Renault driven out on the ice,
and the bonfire, were par for the course,
we thought; we saw straight through them

to the first house as it was with dark
glass set in white and knuckle-dusting walls,
before the burning. We learned to skate fast,

we saw the golden acrobatic fish frozen
under our dissecting blades, the triple-rimmed
eyes open, the stilled quiver of the scales.

We knew how to spin in our own body's compass
and how to vanish, floodlit, in a crowd.
We had by heart the geometries of ice:

the smooth black cross-hatched, pockmarked
brown and frothy white. The gunmetal crack
when it would bear, and the other silence.

We were fluent as the wind until we heard
of drowning, found our pathways undulating
soft as ash along the quick-backed waves.

Incident

Like any other day, the early sun slips
slantwise through the criss-cross railway bridge.

The long-haired, hare-lipped porter counts down
the creosoted tiebars to Worcester and to London;

the gravid schoolgirl in the bunched-up skirt
lolls under anniversary flags and lights a cigarette.

Behind the private parking sign a dog barks
in bursts of three and a plane starts

up from nowhere out of a pale blue sky,
distant and staccato. It is still so early

ants skim fast as waterboatmen along
cracks in the sun-crazed asphalt; the platform

thrums the onrush of the Paddington express
whole minutes before it passes and before the news

comes in, wireless and incredible. At ten the porter
hauls down the bunting. The clustered passengers mutter

and go home, past the dog barking on and on in threes.
It is very still. Smoke-drift scents the wind behind the trees.

Eclogue Over Merlin Street

I

Out of the early morning, the cries of children
rise like gulls, circling, and I startle awake.
They are throwing stones, playing hopscotch.

I remember grids chalked on pavement, a child's
bike buckled, a red scarf spilled. A puddle.
Here the blue voile curtains fall in beautiful veils.

The room settles against them, grows composed.

II

This is home. These are the streets
the terraces and incongruous angles
where we'll arrive and be expected.
Claremont, Merlin, and Amwell –
daily, the long line of repeats,

the terraces and incongruous angles
through basements. The kitchens of
Claremont, Merlin, and Amwell
fronting the reservoir: a grass mound,
half a bicycle, a bank of crocus, railed off.

I remember arriving. Like a migraine
the dark red repeats of the brickwork,
the drummer's off-beat of the rain.

The concrete stairs and their soundings
and my room built into the rooms,
the door and its slow-staged closure, echoing.

The river beds under basement kitchens:
water filtered through our dreams.
Past the reservoir, a great grass mound,
a one-sided square like a hoarding,
where the land marks home, recurrently

as water filtered through our dreams.

There was a building site opposite, a house
just sketched in scaffold, the shouts
of men in hard hats limbering up its

four storeys, pausing at ceiling height,
gesturing single-handed with a plan.

It is for now we live here –
a one-sided square like a hoarding,
the sun mosaiced through a mass of plane trees,
building on the world at our feet

   – for now we live here.

Knocking a nail in, calling for a light.

I watched them cup stars in their hands
and leave with casual disregard for
the future, walking through walls.

This is home, these are the streets
(sun mosaiced through a mass of plane trees)
where we'll arrive and be expected.

From the roof, reputedly, a view of St Pauls.

III

Think of what building builds on.

The triumphal arch, a footprint the size of six houses.
The map of the city you hold in your head, the stairs
where the children hid leading to nothing –

The visitors catch their breath, say a goose, perhaps,
say an angel is passing. They dust down their coats,
check for rain. Tomorrow they are flying home.

Here the scaffolding wraps ladders of glass,
burnished and shot through with atoms of sky.
It is aerial, it points to something else –

The earthbound escalators rise and rise and spill
people (a handbag strap broken, a purple hat, and one
who is lost and twists the tube map round and round).

The hoardings are signed Angel, Angel.

In the plague years this was a burial ground.

IV

This is the texture of home – a limed
birdcage and a real oak swivel chair. The sky
on Sundays looped blue in the calligraphy
of the railings. The scribbled-over sign
for Merlin Street. Each day, it is what I wake to.

I still dream of it, not looking at street signs.
Walking fast, the sky slung like a coat across
my shoulders. Here I negotiate: Cruikshank,
Amwell, Exmouth and the Angel. Faringdon.
Saffron Hill. The silent pointing of the walls.

My husband is working late. He calls,
he says come meet me. We walk home,
his arm in pinstripe curved across my shoulders.
We thread down Rosebery Avenue, join
streams of people passing smoothly between

the taxis, the dazzling side-effects of cars.
The coats over our arms, even our shoulder-
bags have gravity. This is belonging: to walk
in pairs, to pass the repeating pyramids
of streetlights. To cut our own weight in air.

I learn from the façade of the Water Board
this is where the Amwell goes underground.
I think of it as metaphor: it is what we walk on.

V

After the coup they changed the names of the streets.
After the bombing we went to the harbour, saw half
the skyline unchanged, crooked round the same
old Roman fortifications. The water flamed.
We knelt, studied its reflections.

I look for patterns and find them. Long
divisions of plane trees shifting against
the sky, the loose attachments of leaves.

And things that come in threes: his gloves,
the number 19, and the triad of purple figs
we found by a drainpipe in Hardwick Street.

In the fourth house I searched I found a scarred
clock, the hands still turning. A length of blue
tapestry, just slightly scorched. The underside
of a bath above my head. I think of salvage, of hand-
me-downs. A woman sewing under the clock.

Her daughter, hanging the curtains.

VI

Two hundred years ago and from second storey
height in an elm, you might have seen it: St Pauls,
the dome out towards the river, the gold cross lost

in its own reflection: a sun in miniature
and blazing. Sixty years ago you'd have known it
as a black enclosure in the black-out.

I repeat the names of the missing, the streets, the houses.

Now it's not seeing but believing: we trust in
the word for the view that says it is out there,
the dome. The sky whispers over us.

We go by signs: a hiatus in the skyline,
a floodlight down by the river. Pigeons
startling away from a gap in the air.

We say it couldn't happen again, not here.

VII

There was a night I worked late – 3 A.M.
and an acreage of blue muslin ruffled the floor
like the firmament on the third morning:
nebulous, a wake of crumpled, disorderly stars

and a voice on the hour said that this was London.

The bare window showed the room like a star
slowly unfolding the designs of its interior:
newspaper patterns feared 5000 refugees –
like a night thought, like that insomniac

woman opposite pacing the black-out of
the council block across a kitchen window
where fairy liquid lights glowed green and gold.
She moved slowly, like the idea of exile,

like a wise virgin, husbanding her oil.

The papers write about migration: it is not like that.
It is weightlessness. It is walking through walls.

I sat and centred the stars, the floor a drift
of paper and the night sky clear behind the glass.
Thinking the voice in the air could hold us.

It is sitting up to watch a woman across the street
sewing as if it mattered. It is walking upright past
night-lit houses as a carrier for someone else,

for the meaning they would attach, like a star.

London, England, Europe, the World, the Universe.

VIII

My husband slips through the present smoothly
as a fish in its skin. He wakes at 3 A.M., laughing.

He reaches to his full length, yawning, enormous,
his hand splayed against the curtained constellations.

IX

Before there was before and after there was a window
in the thickness of the wall, a twenty-four part
division of panes. A slide-show on the harbour,

the sash shifting across blue, a fishing boat, the prow
with its whorled eye to ward off evil, the hillside
a screed of dust and gorse and rubble, two climbers

angling over the expanse of it towards an afternoon
train that cantilevers the cliff above the divers who
flick through frame after frame on their perpendicular

drop to the grey stone sequences clustered like eggs
nine feet under the hairline fractures of sunlight
that glaze the water while sand on the harbour floor

reflects, reflects and the divers enter into their own
shadows as I step out into the city that maps in perfect
correspondence onto the city in my head.

X

My husband takes me to the window,
shows me the garden scribbled like a footnote,

the glass house caging its sharp green triangles,
and the path past a catslide extension where late sun

skims the roof's tiles and a wind-whiskered tom
stills gravity for a long moment's foothold in the gutter

before plunging like a black note through an octave.

It's not St Pauls, he says, but it's yours if you want it.

He burlesques a pirouette on the terrace.
I blow kisses. A whirlwind of may petals the grass.

XI

At night I wake expecting the pitch of the roof like a tent,
the chalk-dust spiral of the wall five paces to the left.

And then come the sirens, the quick frequencies of the rain.
First light falling powdered as ash. The passing trains.

XII

This is where I walk back from the market.
There was a bike, a red scarf spilled, a puddle.
There were two separate paths down to the harbour.
The hotelier was holding a whole fruit bowl.

There was a bike, a red scarf spilled, a puddle.
I watch the lights come on, the people passing.
The hotelier was holding a whole fruit bowl.
I have lamb, cheese, a loaf of bread, elastic.

I watched the lights come on, the people passing.
At first we threw flowers, white ones, like kisses.
I have lamb, cheese, a loaf of bread, elastic.
The geraniums stood out clearly against the broken glass.

At first we threw flowers, white ones, like kisses.
I lay out oil, figs, rosemary as if they are forever.
The geraniums stood out clearly against the broken glass.
There was a twist of metal by the turn to the harbour.

I lay out oil, figs, rosemary as if they are forever.
This is where I walked back from the market.
There was a flash of metal by the turn to the harbour.
There were two separate paths down.

XIII

My husband says he will teach me London.
We walk on Bankside. We cross at Blackfriars.
This is where his choir met. This is the Tate.

We pass the site of the first doodlebug at Mile End:
the dead weight of a terrace against its shoring,

the squares grassed over, and trains running past
like clockwork. We trace graffiti round the entrance
to St Pauls, chasing the shadows of the names.

These are good days. We kick aside a newspaper
on St John Street: history cockled against the kerb.

We buy a chair and curtain poles, carry them home
past the signs for Angel, Exmouth, and Merlin,
St Pauls View, Amwell Street. Premises to Let.

What the Translator Knows

I

The shape of words like the shadows
of doves, settling. The smooth underside
of the bowl she holds cupped to the light
and the painted fish in it weaving nose

to tail to nose fluid as the contours of this
one word she has lost. The double vision
of fin lapping wing, wing, fin. The surface tension.
The groundswell beneath the metamorphosis.

II

The crack of bone in three different languages.
The words people use when there are no words.
The fine line between *fear* and *panic* and *terror*.
How to blank. How not to put two and two together

when electrodes transmit, transmit, transmit
across the cortex. The mind's reflex instantaneous
as the recoil of a whip (the plaid, the fishweave
pattern). The need to keep silence about it.

All Points North

The arts centre is a former fortress.
Out at sea, it would stand as a beacon,

a pinnacle, a point of aspiration.
It is the visible tip of a labyrinth,

root and canal work deep in the rock
of the island: a last bastion of elliptical

corridors against the enemy slipping
through arrows and in from the bay.

The population of the island is 400,000.
The language is under threat. In a circular

room without windows at the head
of long worn shallows of stairs

we have spent three days and eight tongues
discussing immigration, the *klandestini*:

the rich word summoning hoards
of small boats reeled on a sea shot

with reflections like silk: sardines, cigarettes
and oranges, contraband as metaphor.

As people. Someone doodles a flow chart;
someone complains that is not what he meant

at all. He talks of insurgence, tidal waves.
Outside an aeroplane sounds off the harbour

and we're told of a themed installation
three levels below the bar: a quiverful

of newspaper boats floated on a trickle of ink,
or tar. We claim they are not boats, but birds.

We imagine them there, after lights out, sharp
as arrows, or needles on the point of rotation.

Another Country

Returning, the words were singular as stones
dropped in a still sheet of water, the clear
sense of them sinking under the surface
confusion, the prolific umming and erring.

The roads refused to add up. The school
was a coppice, the field where they'd flown
kites, a mere. There was a wild profusion
of magpies, and everyone was building

something – the prow of a church high
above the river that was the skyline.
Still, there were the vistas, the parks
with small white bridges crossing into an idea

of distance. They were just passing through.
The language returned like an underground
stream to its source: the repeats, the three
recurrent monosyllables to describe the view.

Aubade

Raucously, a gull starts up into the blue.
The chimney like a sore thumb.
If I could tell the story, why would I dance it for you?

A grey cat stalks the edge of the shrubbery,
skedaddles. A woman watches from her balcony,
mouths the line about *dance* and *a wave of the sea.*

Two walkers idle, skimming stones along the bay
with the gravity of non-sequiturs. Testing their weight.
How do I know what I think till I see what I say?

A language student skirts the pebbles before class.
Counts the waves in, counts them out again.

The Printer

Years on, he remembers the letters,
the sense of them, at the very edge
of the fingertips of the mind:

the serifed slimness of *i* and *d*, ligatures
a hunch of shoulders jostling for position –
a *huffiness*. The small sharp hooks of *y*.

He knows the density of space and the diverse
parts of it: the em square, the makeweight
en, the mids and thins and the hair

a silver sliver, a catch in the breath.
He takes his morning paper wedged against
the marmalade, back to front and upside down,

can tell how *a* and *e* go neck and neck,
how the ampersand ends, how the comma
fits to a *t*. And he knows the frequencies –

why Russian stories went in italic,
the perennial scarcity of *k*. He can still
repeat his fingers' dance, analphabetic

over the orders of the tray, the slugs
of lead clicking home, home – but not
how he came here, hurtling into solid

space, slamming the brakes, at sixty,
for a No Entry sign not aimed at him
and wanting the sense of it, the ligature,

the weight of the news in his palm.

The Thought-Pigeon

Imagine a library in summer – the cork, the dust
and the lull of it: the low-level murmur,
the slight ssssh-shifting of stacks of paper
and, at eight times human height, the pink
chequered ceiling.
                    Imagine a pigeon
landing all in an updraft, feet first
on the sill and tumbling over into this
outlandish pool of air.
                  Here it is
on the cornice, rubbing shoulders with Aristotle
and twisting and turning its head with its single
hieroglyphic eye
                     while in ones, twos
and threes the readers glance upwards and
someone asks about a net and someone
confers with the librarian
                    but here it goes again
lumbering the length of the room under
the weight of a sudden loss of sky and the air
creases in its wings like a faulty tent-flap.

Imagine how you could read it: the small
black claw marks on the page, the confined
thought, the laboriousness of flight –

but this is a real pigeon in the wrong place on
a Tuesday afternoon. There is the semi-suppressed
tapping of keyboards. There are eddies and rushes

of concentration. Quietly, the librarian opens
window on window.
                  This is happening now.
And one page it is here, the next it is gone.

Travellers' Tales

I

The cockroaches that night in Jakarta were
superlative, you said: no sleeping
through the click of them, the scurry.

In the morning your mosquito nets were black-
bejewelled, and undulating with antennae
that brought to mind the as-yet-unidentified

species you found your first time of diving
to the sea-bed: nine-armed, and crustacean.
Like a fish twisting in its skin, you stayed

up all night, you said, and the sea-green
shrug of the Atlantic across your shoulders,
the stone houses pitched on its harbour wall,

the high of a red kite singing and slant-
striped bounce of a beach ball all vanished
in the telling. Between us, the deep purple

shellac sheen of discarded mussel backs,
oil on water. Our bone white bowls pearled
with cream, grit, and an enormous barnacle.

II

Though for you these things would be too close
to home, sheet-metal dolphins round the balustrade
on the balcony of my fourth-floor hotel room

and puffed-up pigeons edge the corbels.
The sky's sea-blue over a terrace of keystone
borders and saucers set for a cat with tortoise-

shell-tarred paws. On the hour, six bells ring
from the Church of the Salvation of St Paul
over a town heaped like a quarry, inverted.

Tonight fricatives, plosives and labials
of some foreign argument round out
the ventilation shaft, and the room is adrift

on its soundings. With five seas between us,
I'll invent for you the dancing on the terraces.
The loose cannon and flares from Roman

candles that spin awkward backflips and fold
inward like dying stars. The slow resounding
retort that staggers distantly to my senses.

Jetlag

The curve of the path is off-kilter. The door jambs
tilt their weight against the key as it hefts the lock
and distances chafe between overgrown grasses.
The hall is dark as a looking-glass.

On the table a bowl full of apples shrunk beneath
their skins and stippled black with long exposure.
The air is three-dimensional; shoals of dust flow
and ebb across the stairs, where on the wall

the whole of August waits to be torn off.

I'm out of keeping. If I turn back fast enough
I'd catch you through the purling transparency

of the Atlantic as through a window, reaching
to the dresser with a swimmer's slow motion
for the compact or comb I left behind.

Three Takes on a Location

Take 1

A stone's throw across the valley from
the town (steep terraces and an abandoned
campanile) there is the villa. Shuttered,

and nothing special, you say, just a stone
frieze of the moon and stars, a shell-
shaped basin. And a bridge

like an aqueduct marching on the first floor
entrance hall, and five people walking
round it, shaking stones from their shoes,

leaning and pointing across the balustrade.
The sun-crushed smell of bay. Under their feet,
the architect's imagination set in stone:

the arched, the orchestrated air.

Take 2

At the foot of the hills a ring
of tombs, Etruscan, cut from the stone.
Hollow as gaps in the memory.

We touch the altars, the alcoves.
What to make of them?

The farmer out among his beanstalks
with a broad-brimmed hat and
wheelbarrow is neither here nor there.

Take 3

Like a portrait without light behind the eyes,
three barred windows deep in the rockface.

The subterranean chapel of Mithras.
The chapel of the Virgin.

A priest raises his hands to the hill-
bearing columns, the traces of illumination:
St Christopher and Mary, repeatedly,

with dark-rimmed eyes, watching and fading.

The plaster on the floor.

And here we are walking above it all.

The avenue opens as if we'd been around before,
clutching awkward fistfuls of blackberries,

scuffing last year's leaves while the crickets
idiomatically turn over two disjointed notes.

Coda

Evening on the mountain: landfall made
visible in the ridgebacks of foliage:
the darks and darker stills.

The sky blue, the firs like pointers.
The sun setting in silver pintucks across the lake.
You could say it is raw material.

You could say it is.

On Liking Glass Houses:

the untidy ones, skewed down gardens like an accident
with a log pile, windows for hindsight, or wedged
anyhow in the angle between hedge and railway line.

The way their emptiness invites a pause,
the way a sinuous movement against the glass
resolves into a cat weaving through iris

as if spooled down a thread: the length of
its spine an updraft of single hairs fine enough
to paint themselves a perfect likeness.

                                        Years ago

on the canal you passed a studio, an old man
lifting gold leaf on a comb of badger's hair,
holding his breath as the boat's wake ran

clopping gently along the wooden wall of the shed.
And you held your course past the ironworks
and the cemetery, through lock over lock

but thought back and gave a name to it: *illumination.*

You remember that now, out on the edge of town
where a woman has walked into the room holding

an almost spherical pot of jam: the ruby globe
of the word rolled on the tip of the tongue,
and the sense of likeness, of trying it out for size.

Vista

(for Lucy, after Edward Thomas)

Legend has it, it was the answer to a prayer
after years of careful construction on weights
and pulleys of borrowed syntax, lines

of thought running like the black bands
and fretwork of Victorian gothic to display
a niche, a clause:
                        suddenly the poem

sufficient unto itself as the long minute's
view when a train pauses between stations,
the country one part earth to six parts air

and the white house in its clean timber
frame clear and open as if it stood alone
and unlooked-for. Or so they say.

House Painting

In miniature

The wall's coarse whitewash is overcast,
shadows itself
               under the startling black of the gutter
               the scissoring shade of pyracantha:
the thorn, the pointed leaf, and the single berry.

Imagine it, just two inches away, and waxing:
a globule of blood on an outstretched finger,
the elliptical dint of the light.

The resonances of it.

In watercolour

The first thing is the curve of the horizon, drawn
round three sides of the sheet of paper and tied
tight as a bow.

Then the thick of the hills, like cumulus, sloping
off as the ink runs into furrows under the strong
black H of the water tower.

On middle ground, a bad wobble in the fence stands
for the sound of the railway, the trains shunting or
pulling in to Exeter, Exeter St Davids –

Yellow is for the sun, and the dog down the hill
quick in its kennel behind the blackthorn
and barking diffusely.

Close up, silver is the pear's knotty mass, the flipped
undersides of eucalyptus leaves, and the five
stone steps that run between them

to the dead end where moss is for green channels
of fern and undergrowth like fur the texture
of rabbit's ears, a pad of paper.

The terrace underfoot is concrete, a sketchy affair.
As for the house, you have your back to it:
it is where you start from.

In wood

Under the bead of light that tracks down the two
dimensions of a spider's web, the wood
is a dark medium.

Under the rose, along the enormous deckle
of a leaf-edge an eye-sized ant carries the three
parts of its body

like an exercise in articulation, arched
gloss black over all the miscellaneous
textures of afternoon

and whole hours go into its making:

the way into the wood seen feelingly,
like returning by night through the close-
grained dark and reeling

off the hill by touch alone: the sole-stippling
gravel, domes of moss, and the gate's long splinter
splitting across

the small brushstrokes of the privet and the pressing
detail, like that urn in the porch, the grit of it
to fingers dragging down the scales.

In motion

This film is so old it shows the texture of the air
like canvas woven in and out of the action

which happens very slowly.
                              Two hands set down
a tray where the teacups jitter and spill

light and someone in shorts bends stiffly over
the double-crossed joints of a folding chair,

tests the accidental, unmatched patch in the grey
seat, which was orange, and calls to mind the story

behind it, that Sunday when Uncle John fell through.

It is all odd angles. It is thin as the block-patterned
tablecloth that blows into the frame and freezes –

and behind it there is laughter carrying on like music
in a room where the piano has just stopped playing:

there's the father who conjured coins from your ear,
the mother who changed the shapes of shadows

in passing, sun filtered through the squares of her
black and white check dress, the solid shaft of her hair.

In the dark

A child edging forward the broad blunt scissors across
a sheet of black wax crackled on a thin film of paper.

Running with it up the concrete steps to the house,
to show the colours: the red and gold bicycle,

the white horse traced with careless fluency,
the sudden iris flagging her black front door.

Auricular

The first night home we leave the windows open.
The dark shifts softly as a curtain in its frame
while bats come out, swiftean

and irregular as the thin edge of a prayer
sounding the pitch of the gable, the timbre
of the slatted fence, and quicker

than compass needles in the crossfire of responses.

We imagine the inaudible exchange, remember
our train stretching the length of the coast

to the length of an afternoon, stopping and
starting down the line south from the mountains,
the soundtrack like a running question

and the leaden echo of all the intervening towns.

The bats flick darkly past invisible and familiar barns,
make current the spaces between the solids.

Young Girl with a Flute

(circle of Vermeer)

I am uncertain, unattributable.
My face half shadowed by a saucer
hat, striped – the lilt of it.
One of my eyes, far away.

They call my right hand clumsy, say
the whole portrait, if it is one,
is like a large chest awkwardly
jammed across a door frame.

Light falls in diagonals, in a barricade.
Behind it, my flute rests against the table
while I talk to someone over your shoulder.
I have it loosely at my fingertips,
two of the stops just visible.
Don't we all need distraction, the hills?

The Poet with Pen and Ink

If I could run a thin black line round the rosehip's
orange-tinted berries, touch their bulbousness
with crimson at the base and ink the curvature
of the stem, catching the highlights that break
like white road markings going round the bend –
if I could pin down a blunt, stocky thorn before
taking off into the wild attack of Russian vine,
all flourish and blot with just one leaf in detail,
double-edged with sun against the spearhead of
a single railing or the pediment's long diagonal

that suggests there is something behind it all,
I'd escape the hunt for the cadence of the pines,
the changing light and the small rustle of things
falling through the trees, the empty husk
of the hazelnut three out of every four years.
If I could narrow it down to a single line

linking one thing to another, the way next door
hang out their washing between a hook in the fence
post and the gutter and that bush starry with haws.

Ode to an empty flat

Beginning is difficult.
It is clear what's behind sticks of furniture.
The wall exists to shadow the chair.
The chair is a fistful of uprights against the wall.

Still, each thing has its own distinction.

The head of a paintbrush has its set number of sleek
black hairs before it floods with a single purpose.

There is a cause that lifts the coir matting twice over.

And there is something to be said even for the one
cedarwood mothball that runs across the wardrobe
shelf and falls as a grey stone falls plumb
to the bottom of an inlet, settles in its outline.

The two rooms resonate with it.

After dark, cats cry in tongues twisted so sharp
the sound's something you could get a handle on.

Icarus on Earth

(2005)

From this the poem springs: that we live in a place
That is not our own and, much more, not ourselves
And hard it is in spite of blazoned days.

WALLACE STEVENS,
'Notes toward a Supreme Fiction'

By the Book

When he came to tell her, she went to the library.

It was early. She could think a path through the day
like an aisle running the length of the reading-room
like a finger tracked down the dust of the open shelves
like blood circulating in the body's glove.

He watched the paint blister on the door to Admissions.

She found the three things she wanted under Fable
with tight calf spines. With the palm of her hand
she smoothed out the rucked pages as wind
flattens a pond. She took up her pen.

He placed his head between his hands against the flat
of the wall. It was like talking to a stone, he said.

She sat by the window and translated: *Child,*
did you not see the pike in the reeds? – that was why
we flew. Did you not see the hawk? Her mind
vaulted like sunlight off a pigeon's back.

He looked at the towers and the twist of the stairs
taking up the argument the way a pen takes up ink.
He heard footsteps and laughter: it was the librarian.
Darkly, a pigeon cut an inverse parabola in air.

And when it struck six and they came to lock the gates
and he left without speaking, she was translating:
Carissimi, most beloved, you should know that these things
signify – And stopped. And smiled, thinking of him vaguely
as an undercurrent in the soft skein of water across
her wrists, and how the sentence would go on the next day.

Origami

Boat

This is the third principle
after plane and steeple.
It goes against the grain –

it takes diagrams. First
square, then circle, it is
a buckler, a catch-all,

a pocketful of air or
the talismanic paper-weight
that won't sink but like

a dance song, fable without
moralitas, the get-out clause
of a year and a day or the sea-

bound sieve that's the final
cat-like leap of faith
bobs over the dotted line and away.

Fox and Rooster

Go back a long way, snout
to beak, barking up a tree
or pacing a short space

of riverbank. Looking to lay
to rest their differences. Led
astray by their own shadows.

As once the fox, thinking to put
a stop to this vaunting parodist
made off with the rooster across

his back – but when the cock crew
and the woman ran out with a torch
what he saw in silhouette against

the barn wall was the rooster
bearing a fox like a cowl. He knew
then there'd be no clean end to it.

Cat

Demanding never less than perfection –
first the steep pitch of the ears, then
six sharp creases for the shoulder-bones –
all to poise it to turn its back.
And whiskers? This is the difficult one.

Guitar

No, but this – imagine the necessary
size of the sheet of paper. In so far
as there are guidelines, their scale

is one to one, so here you are,
crawling uncharted territory with pins
and scissors and string, looking for

the beginning marked *you are here*
because – while you've approximated
neck and belly before – balance and voice

are new entirely. So here you are
on the floor, folded experimentally over
the polished surface like an interpreter

of the dark song of the waves against
a wooden hull and the fine flicker of
a cat's whisker, its radar re-tuning.

Bird

So, on the third day, when the sun set
into the sea as if there were no tomorrow
and the waves had tongues like bells

he cast it out. Its smooth white sides
ruffled paper-light between his palms.
First, it was hesitant as if there might be

a new end to the story, but then it
cut straight as faith, or a plane:
they had only to wait. And when

it came again, dark against the sun
as a chink to swallow the ocean
its wings were warped with a map

of the country they'd left behind,
and from its beak they unravelled
a key and a length of red twine.

Elayne

Some things the book doesn't mention –
the way she would walk the walls daily
and compass the horizon, Brittany

beyond it, and beyond that, island upon
island to the edge of the world walled
like a garden. Or how she'd woken

that night, to hear his breathing turn
like a change in the weather, swell
of a slack sail, the first whisper of rime

on a ripened fruit's skin, and saw him
adrift in the sheets, straight and naked
as a needle. And saw the shape of his

dreams, something like a ship's bow-wave
going on ahead, and saw, because love
was different then, how he'd think of her,

if at all, as the catch and drag of her skirt,
life's element of resistance: the skin
of an apple to the teeth, frostbitten grass

to the feet, a horse's straw-sweet breath
in air, or hawk in crewel work: like
the thing he lacked. And how she'd be

the heavier for it, but for all that, how
they'd have twinned, his idea and hers,
like sail and wind, wind and wing,

if life had been different then. Or still
like tapestry and needle: the turning
under, and the stitching in.

Proverbial

Twice now, this road. So the sign
at the crossing has a familiar slant
and ashes are beside themselves under
a weight of leaves that last visit were

nerve-ends, the first lines in history.
You've settled here lightly, the way
a river runs together all the places
it passed. And if we correspond

it's as water parts into umber, lapis,
terracotta, all the colours of the earth –
as, looking back, you'll see someone
catching the sun on a wide, amphibious

verandah, and see your way clear
to the inlet, the stepping stones, to taking
your life in your hands and crossing here.
And the way it is not the same river.

Icarus on Earth

Mother

A kind of metamorphosis. His arm
twists fishlike through my fingers,
he lives outside, cries like a gannet,
shears through raspberry canes
and pampas grass for whole Sundays
shuttered in the tree-house. The cat
comes in feathered and tarred.

Still worse, the things I've overheard:
how he one-legged along the parapet,
head skied, arms spread-eagled, and
trainspotting, he said, till they talked
him down. And now, when I bend
to kiss him I see in the August blue
of his eyes not myself, inverted, but

a soft flicker as when we swim
under the viaduct: joint jack and kick
of our long-legged spines, overarm
reaches parting doubled nets of birch
and the rush a kind of cradling.
Tap and pulse of our feet against
the current's shaled strata invisible

till he lights out in a rivulet
arrowhead, a catch in my body's
smooth casket waving
from the bridge and I
am watching the sky webbed
and sinuous between his fingers,
arms flexed to my sides,

treading water like lead.

Girl

What I remember is this: the afternoon
running out in long grasses, the quick white
root system of our fingers and their slender
hold on the earth, the afterlife of the worm.

The word *loam*, the sharp sand edging
the pit, ten strong carapaces of nails chocked
with grime: digging for Australia, digging
for the island, and up to the elbows in it.

The bird's eye view: cavern of dock leaves,
borage a masthead startled through
the ribbing and into skyblue gravity over
my nose and cheekbone among reeds

in the pond, a leg kicking between branches.
Caustic grain of brick against the skin
and on my knee an exopthalmic jewel
of blood, a toad's eye darkling. Arc

and spring of the pearl-handled penknife
in my palm. On the wide stone ledge
static of a dragonfly breaking its flight.
The pelt of sunlight ruffled on my back.

Icarus

As it is in books, when, Friday afternoons,
the plimsoll-footed teacher hands down
reading time and the four walls
of the classroom quiver and fall
away as a springboard clappers, a diver
soars, or the father comes home
from the factory and brings a kite,
perfect strung wings,

and the long lines of print glide and brim
like gulls in formation or in battery:
waves over a dazzle of white whose
wax-coated covers take to the hands
like wings so my feet are digging the soft
sift of sand, the sharps of shellfish.
I've a graft of feathers like tattoos
under the skin,

the taut of struts in a kite's casing
as it lifts: a ribcage of air,
a mote skied in the stairwell on
its ascent long and stepped as a lifeline
when I turn from the page as from the world
under my wing as if there were no known
end to it, when the kite castles in air as if
there were no strings.

Girl

What I remember is this –
that you called me in the long fall-out
of an autumn Sunday, the kiss

of leaves turning in the park, creak
of branches the leather hinging of rooks
on take-off or the sign for Welwyn, Palmer's Green.

How we were on top of the world
and our shadows' crossed purposes, trod the earth
under and fell windstopped

and laughing at the top of the escarpment.
How the common ground cut below the pale
as if there'd be no end to it and

the train on the viaduct beneath our feet
shook up the green as the wind
pulses through long grasses and we

hung against post and rail in diapason
giving slip to its slipstream. How
we went under and drew the sun

down and round with us. It was
early dark. Like a meteor a train
came out over the moon and rattled the stars

from Orion. You knew a way out,
you said; you said you walked all night
with the feathers I gave you twisting about

and about again against your palm
like radar, a rudder, the two-pronged
wooden fork of divination.

Now you write with the weight of the Atlantic
behind you that even the stars look different.
So I could tell you I hunch the height

of ocean against the skyline, that I drove
out tonight and the streetlights spun
constellar over the road.

That I would give you the earth
in a handful of signs, tilt against Kansas, Illinois:
Hitchin, Hertford, Hatfield and the north.

Biographer

If it had been a different island, less green,
less grey. If there had been no hedges, no
litany of trains fluent in the liquid
air, no rain cradling the echo as a bubble
about to burst. No movement. No past.
No Sundays in the greenhouse taking up
roots and putting them down again.
If it had been a different cross-section
of earth against the glass. If the laws of
gravity had gone west, if there'd been
no books to tell us about them, vicarious,
flipped pages dipping like island on
island below the horizon, prodigal as if
there'd been nothing new under the sun:
island on island dipping below the horizon,
flipped pages prodigal to tell us about them.
Or if there'd been no books to show how
the balled earth bends gravity to its laws.
If the crossing had been sectioned off,
the sun past movement behind glass.
No. Sunday a greenhouse, a cradle,
a bubble about to burst in the rain.
Putting down roots and taking them up,
the air liquid, and fluent as an echo
its litany of grey, hedges, green
going west with the trains, vicarious –
no less if it had been a different island.

Girl

Tonight you say you'll be flying, and to Phoenix,
and this, I suppose, is the film played slow,
the myth swung into reverse as waves, wing-
backed, break to release you as you plumb
skyward, feathers dart to their appointed arms
and the quiver of wax hardens: there was

no fall. And so you head west, grave
as an owl in daylight, and if on descent
the plains are starred with cacti, a near
subliminal pricking of thumbs, you'll stall:
balance the compact earth beneath your feet,
clap up dust from your wings, say you flew direct.

Icarus

Don't think I've forgotten
smoke rings of your laughter rising,
grasses planed overhead.
The back of your hand a chart.

Smoke rings of your laughter rising
under the skylight of the viaduct
The back of your hand a chart:
a ridgeway, four possible compass points

under the skylight of the viaduct.
Two hundred to one, you're on
a ridgeway, four possible compass points;
islands flatten the earth,

two hundred to one, you're on.
The script is copperplate and clear:
islands flatten the earth
as if cliffs marked horizons;

the script is copperplate and clear
as if there were no beginnings.
As if cliffs marked horizons,
ambition vaults like the line between pylons.

As if there were no beginnings,
the snatch of song from a car on the coast road.
Ambition vaults like the line between pylons –
A Domine, Domine.

The snatch of song from a car on the coast road
A cappella without words:
A Domine, Domine
And the coast was clear.

A cappella without words,
the steep staged updraft of ascent,
and the coast was clear
as if we all knew the end of it:

the steep staged updraft of ascent,
lichens and the rumour of trains in my head.
As if we all knew the end of it,
the giddy height of the skyline under the bridge,

lichens and the rumour of trains in my head.
Don't think I've forgotten
the giddy height of the skyline under the bridge,
grasses planed overhead.

Daedalus

Since I had my books and the future
hadn't happened yet, I figured flying
in the face of history: went west, of course,
but early, the birth of my son
unheralded, and even his begetting
unattended to. I meant to give myth

the slip easily as I first moulded myth-
ology as a labyrinth. As if the future
had no strings, I came without getting
a picture of this island, took its trains, flying
machines, and grey-green lichens for my sun,
my own inventions, its matter-of-course

High Streets and Sundays for a new course
in life, and swopped the old myth
for the new: married and had a son.
And so he grew and demanded the future
for his own: fierce as Orion flying
off the handle, he couldn't help forgetting

the limits on his rebellion. Regretting
his island life, he traced my abandoned course
in books, absorbed astronomy. The night-flying
owl's cut-out against the stars was a myth
blotting the view. Tense, he saw the future
as his backdrop. He was my son.

In short, he took his course to the sun
for one of his own begetting, flying
for the sky blue future, and falling into myth.

Given time again, I'd choose a different sun,
ocean, age, and island without regretting
my loss of flight and still the future –
would it stoop on us, its collision course
the bull's eye of eclipse? They say myth
grants metamorphosis, the sudden flying

start, but I can't forget that I was flying
for our lives, or how I thought my sun
would guide me from the true north of myth
and the end I was always for getting.
Today the vapour trails are hopelessly off course.
Still a plane scribbles, heads or tails into the future.

Eye-witness

What they don't tell is that he was burning
up as he fell, like a paper spill
twisting from a bonfire
and his naked arms still feathering.

So he met the ground lightly, on
an updraft, his first steps gargantuan,
rebounding. Having seen from above
the world was round he meant to get

to the bottom of it. The horizon dimmed
into further horizons. Later, on the cliff
it wasn't footprints they found but shafts
of primaries, carbonised, chasing the earth.

Biographer

After, he forgot what hit him,
traced the marks under his skin

with a puzzled finger but never asked;
put aside the feathered shaft

that broke from his shoulder-bone
and was never quite at home

in the sun, but would start
at his coiled shadow as at a mark

of interrogation. He preferred
indoors, took to watching birds

from the picture window, wide-
fingered, was known as the shy

ornithologist who studied Greek
and islands and wouldn't speak

of them – though hieroglyphs in his books
he said reminded him of rocks

cascading to an expanse of sand
like waves and a man

slanting across them, a slight talk
in the swing of his arms as he walked.

Girl

What I'll remember is this:
the plum-dust surface of your desk,
a cat's angular silhouette.
Shadowed carriages of a waltzer
rising stilted as wing-beats in eschalon
against the wall.
              The sky-blue room
swinging up and over under
a ride's kaleidoscopic siren
song, and answering yes, you are
the spring in sprung rhythm, the glide
in elision, the high in the five
minute warning. The flight in flying
buttress, the pink in sky-blue, kick
in a suspension bridge and suspension
of disbelief. The swing in calypso,
the ground cut from under my feet –

And naming you Icarus.

Let's start again, let slip
the distraction of wings at your back,
trajectories buckled down and under
the rule of thumb, the necessary
ending: say there's history
and horizon enough in the waltzer
ascendant on the wall and writing
a kind of metamorphosis.

Crystal Palaces

Because there are three stones in a whorled glass
shell in the bathroom. Because the light is grey.

Because there is a pelt of may and snow petals
across the panes. Because the wind has a shard-

like edge to it; because the reception is poor.
Because in Gordon Square a puddle blacks out

the cracks in the paving so your step skims
the jagged plane tree rotated through 180

degrees and the aircraft between its branches.
Because we have both seen these things,

at different times, and the way the suburban
line tunnels into Kings Cross and spills over

till under the cut glass web the platform
surges like a mackerel catch and splinters

into London. Because it's hard to make visible
connections, but there used to be gardens

up that line. Improvised darts, the wreck
of a greenhouse. A thrush's anvil in moss.

Because I saw you reading. So we stood
for hours outside the library without speaking.

So they are rebuilding the pier at Brighton.
So you sing at night in your house between

the trees with the windows uncurtained,
and can be seen passing among the branches.

So I have your voice cupped in the shell
of the telephone; so a plane touches down,

a skimmed stone skips below the pier.
So we spell out the silvered hieroglyphs

of life-lines against the glass, doubled up
and amazed at our luck as at the glimpsed

sign near Alexandra Palace that claims trains
may run on either line in both directions.

Floating Poem

I give you the summer – evenings, salt on the lip
of two blue-green glasses, and heat viscous
as the citrus twist in a highball. Like abroad,
echoes up the marble stairwell to your flat,
the spyhole, the static on the entry-phone,
the smell of cat. The carrying back a whole
net of lemons. Like abroad, too, sleeping beside
ourselves in the long light hours while outside
someone called the shots in that everlasting
game of tennis, and the cats drifted in and out
of our consciousness, saw fair play from tiers
of flowerpots on the balcony, or skittered
the corridor like a shot of ice that twists from
the fingers and containing glass, through open
doors and out, into the Bombay sapphire sky.

Mythography

On South Street, a bookshop, a hat exchange
A sleek grey cat countered in its box
A first time for everything
Tin-gilt angels in mosaic frames

A sleek grey cat countered in its box
History repeats itself
Tin-gilt angels in mosaic frames
A clear case of overcrowding

History repeats itself
Blue shades of a café, spinach and eggs
A clear case of overcrowding
Rococo spindles on a floor like glass

Blue shades of a café, spinach and eggs
The first time of asking
Rococo spindles on a floor like glass
A pretzel twist salt on the tongue

The first time of asking
Small effects of estrangement
A pretzel twist salt on the tongue
Barnes & Noble and the Liberty Bell

Small effects of estrangement
Repeats playing hot and cold
Barnes & Noble and the Liberty Bell
The slick grey Delaware and bridge, suspended

Repeats playing hot and cold
Legends intuited across a bell's broken rim
The slick grey Delaware and bridge, suspended
In between the planes keep on landing

Legends intuited across a bell's broken rim
The old country's tongues of fire and plague
In between the planes keep on landing
We buy Jonson and a book of mythography

The old country's tongues of fire and plague
On Society Hill, the belles in organza
We buy Jonson and a book of mythography
We say we'll have this cyclical time no longer

On Society Hill, the belles in organza
Plane trees are leading the great west window
We say we'll have this cyclical time no longer
We slip through lightly as oil on water

Plane trees are leading the great west window
On South Street, a bookshop, a hat exchange
We slip through lightly as oil on water
A first time for everything

Valediction

Island-bound, the things I leave you with:
a coast road out of season, land down
to a bar of low pressure between sea

and ocean and the light mercury
stopping each boulevard. The spring
in the boardwalk, wire-wrapped roller

coaster track, and the striped awnings.
A want of interiors: wood drifts from
dormers, masts through windows shifting

in and out of alignment and the sky
jarred between boarding-house turrets.
All the spiralled escape routes,

the sidewalk barred, the finned
Cadillac we never hired, our amphibean
shadows. The boardwalk flexing

like bones in our hands' skin, a strong
undertow of desire. An abiding
distrust of countries without a coastline.

Clairvoyance

Spring, and the river is rising: claxon
of geese, shrill of forsythia's five
stems forked in a glass jar,
and wavering. An oak sprouts waterfalls,

the house paw-talks in the roof at night,
there are toothmarks in the butter.
Industrious, bees batten on the carpet,
the upholstery, signing like mutes,

and rain nets me in. Your messages slip
through with arrowed wakes, migratory
in formation. You say there's snow,
you've banked an enormous fire,

have been out walking among the trees
I couldn't name, gauging their sextant angles
with the measured glance of a fisherman.
That you'll drive by another river, fetch

bread, jalapenos, liquor. Unpacking,
the brown paper bag spells contraband;
in your glass room the whisky glows
amber through a forest in silhouette

like fish bright among water-weed,
the current under ice. It will be late there.
Here tower bells tumble as turbines.
You'll be heaping up coals before sleeping.

I open all the windows. Early light
rimes the bees' carpet of fur.

Kitty's Song

*Now that Fire is the Radix of Life evidently appears from the
following Experiment: Let a Cat and a Candle be put together
in an Oven...and you will perceive that the Instant the Candle
goes out, that Instant the Cat dies.*
RICHARD SYMES,
Fire Analysed (1771)

Observe the cool, the empirical
certainty that knows each soul
has a housing and fire
belongs in ovens. That science
can't breathe the air of metaphor

but grasps at the soft blue quiver
of flame distilled to a vital spark
on the flatbed floor of the oven.
They'd have to pan for it:
it wouldn't stir a feather.

Still, too quick for the dead
hand of the recorder, when
they come to break the seals
and bury the evidence, it slips
like metaphor or a slim burglar

headfirst through an eye-patch
window and comes to rest
among flowerpots on a ledge
where you find me catlike,
and ready for rehousing.

And if you take me in,
I shall burn like a night-light.
I shall consider the premises
dispassionately as a moth
in a candle. I shall inhabit you

as I inhabit my own skin.
Sometimes I'll be domestic,
slack on the sofa as an unbent
bow, but nights, or when I
sense the pressure of a door

or window shutting me in,
my swansdown fur will ruffle
blue as metaphor as I observe
the rites of the corridor, rake out
the embers in my throat, and sing.

Oxygen
(for PJB)

I

It's in the off-white squares of the plan
for the new house, the two whole bedrooms,
half-moon doors, and five children

poring over it. In grass to bare feet,
the steep of garden falling
to a stream, curl of petticoats

on take-off and laced shadows
of blackcurrant leaves. A shifting
geometry of air in the spin

of cricket balls, the lime and lilac
cage of the mantel, in your mother's
warning and the flame and the way

you give it tongue, this life, like
the first breath of sun on the metal
rim of a liner in dry dock, crescent

with promise, repeatedly.
And later, in the rise and fall of
Southampton Water, abstractedly

opening a window from the sick-
room for the view, a breathing space:
the hills' self-containment above

a riot of small boats like the one
you joked of owning: the quick of it,
the flying white of its wake.

II

Glory is a bicycle in June
Queen Anne's lace pointilliste edging the hollow lane
and the sky flying like fabric treadled from a machine

in fits and starts, the earth's curve
rising through your spine, the spinning wheel
whistling a hole in the air and closing it behind.

Is land enough for a house grafted pouch
by seed-head pouch and yours for the husbanding,
sunspots like sparks flying upwards, kretch

of gravel or the pause on the horizon
brow of the hill as a trout steadying itself
against the stream by the pulse of its tail,

flicker of gills its near-imperceptible breathing
before the plunge, the wake rising effervescent,
the sky's pierced blue carillon.

III

Close as the roughened reverse of embroideries,
the garden a needling of pine,
the chestnut-knuckled earth.
Root-system of the back of the hand, weeding,
and at the back of the mind, the house

clear as a bell in the forest's sussuration.
Close as the roughened reverse of embroideries
the overspill of a piano scales
the chestnut-knuckled earth,
wooden flats of conkers and croquet.

Steps on the crazy paving, a white dress
clear as a bell in the forest's sussuration
at twilight, twigs backing up the sky.
The overspill of a piano, scales
branching into a nave, a steeple.

The house light as a leaf in the clearing:
steps on the crazy paving, a white dress
(a flame turned up high, iridescent) iris
at twilight. Twigs backing up the sky,
a hand against the glass on the landing,

the solid oak boards treading air
(the house light as a leaf in the clearing).
Oil husbanded in the Aladdin lamp:
the flame upturned high (iridescent, iris)
catching against lichens on the sill, fingers

fluttering nave and steeple against the glass,
the solid oak boards. Treading air,
the passing bulk of the white horse Casablanca –
like oil husbanded in the Aladdin lamp,
the story of his bolting, like twigs, lichens, moss
adrift at the back of the mind. Like the house.

IV

It's in the all-clear each morning
at five, taking the deep green
steps down into the day, in

the silence of the house brimming
over a hymn's skyline –
the first three bars of it startled

through light-dividing banisters and
the spun silk sheets of the air,
rising
   my mind to me

Is in the setting, the children's
boats, soda-powered, rocking in
their basin, in the crescent

half moons of teacups running
estuarine as a train's passage
cradles the house on its foundations.

Is knowing that down the line
they've taken away the sandbags
at Eastleigh; that when at night

the moon in the black-out beyond
the black-out soars like a voluntary
over the deep central well of the house

the lamp in your hand mounts steadily
to meet it as your voice in the kitchen
rounds – *my spirit sang all day* –

like a naked flame against the glass.

V

As if it were still possible to see you
each evening upright at the polished oak
uprights of the gate-legged table
and turning up the lamp to enter
in the bright excluding circle the detail
of the day's expenditure as if
when you fill the sleek blue pen with
your left hand, then with your right
record in flourishing italic *Tuesday,*
5 April, it's not the dry goods
you're intent upon, the tea, flour,
sugar, strong tape to mend apron,
not even the rare walking shoes,
pink beads for Mary, or the discovery
that after the doctor's fee, steak,
eggs, there is still, at the week's end,
a shilling to spare: no, it's rather
as if, cycling home from Lyndhurst
or Romsey you saw the road an almost
Roman swathe through the forest and
saw it carry on – past the railway bridge,
the first tomatoes in the greenhouse,
the cat Toto extended the length of the garage
wall under the window where you pause,
passing upstairs, to turn the brass
candlestick, glance across the orchard
and even then rub out a mark on
the glass deftly as if crossing a seven,
rounding an eight or a nought
and smiling quietly as if the day's
total had come up even –
as if it would ever have been possible
to see you in private, as if, if anyone
had called – Alan fretful, a child unwell –
you wouldn't have closed the figure
and closed the accounts, and gone
to meet them smiling as if what you
were about was of no importance.

VI

As if the diver at the high
point of the fish-tail could
angle that way forever, you watch

the whole world spun in the slow
embrace of her overarm as she
swings into the downdraft,

a slip of the air to the cool
blue interlace marking the spot
where she enters quietly as if

into your house in darkness with
a twist smooth as the key
turning home, the indrawn

hands with a pulse like breathing in
the lavender scent-and-textured
hall and small globes streaming

between the fingers on her fluid
double-jointed progress to
the viewing-glass. Crystalline

in an all-over halo she hangs
there in suspension
mouthing a sentence perfect

round and incomprehensible as
the weight of this radiance,
jewel-like, when she slowly

lifts herself to the ladder where
the water is open sesame
and shut again –

And here you are leaving, taking
your grandchild by the hand,
walking quietly back to the station.

VII

It is in the late move to the coast
the singularity of waking alone
impromptus to Paignton and Norwich
the day arched like a dome
overhead, the keening of seabirds

Sundays in church, polyphonic
in the hush before the voluntary.
The singularity of waking alone
in the long lift of the morning
walking the cliff-top level

with the thick caps of trees
and gull-backs breaking like waves
in the hush before the voluntary
sussuration of the sea between leaves
in the long lift of the morning

the flying white lace of a handkerchief
scent of home – lavender, polish, leather –
and gull-backs breaking like waves,
fringed barbs rising on each long-drawn breath.
Sussuration of the sea between leaves

the recapitulation, blue-black letters
written evenings in the lamplight
scent of home – lavender, polish, leather –
in the air between the fingers waving, at last,
fringed barbs rising on each long-drawn breath,
the open window in the hospital room.

Patience
(for Peter)

A wooden sea, cobalt
and gilt breakers agitating

on the spot, rocking
horses. A Scots

pine in a storm or, indoors,
the tabby's fine black barcode rising

and falling on its breath,
the cabinet painter in an angle-

poised halo tipping the froth
with his sable on

every third ascender and the crow's
feet in the crow's basket, the brush

lavishing more gold on each
line than it can possibly bear

while the lookout raises a light, Jonah
in the whale's ribbed cage circles

cautiously, a matte bruise
under the dogtooth burnisher like the sails

of gold leaf the rag of a leaf's
rag and bone, no more twist –

Listening for the voice banked
in the clouds, some kind of transference,

working the brush to a point
for the whale uprising dark

as houses on the skyline,
a twist in its tail ravelling

up all the broad equivalences:
the cat in its cradle, waves

withdrawing from the tabby-tongued sand,
the two-stroke ship in the middle distance.

A dog in the barn setting up a howl,
creak of wet wood as the storm door closes.

Translation

(for Gertrude)

I

It is a house with a bay,
windows the grained green
of total immersion.

The sea beyond the glass.
It is the three steps down
to the workroom, is lifting

aside the crewel curtain heavy
with the twenty-six animal
letters of the alphabet, squared.

It's the cursor's rapid pulse
in a half-dark room,
it's setting out in a snowstorm

for the pier rehearsing
synonyms for lighthouse –
beacon, watchtower, *vuurtoren* –

as if they were fine white crumbs
leading home. It's having the senses
doubled: ten inward wits, twenty

digits. It's having two black birds
to eat from your palms.
And it's child's play –

chalk over cracks in the paving,
a whole afternoon's expedition to
the cave across the bay.

It's finally losing your bearings,
the quay awry in a snowflake
miasma. It's the twist of glass

that centres a marble: the heart
of the matter, the slipper sense
of things ravelled at the root.

II

We might have said, it is like
flight, like hedging your doubts –
the cliff-face exposure, the harsh white

gutturals of screed and sea and bird
and the scrabble for a foothold –
the long too-much of the world

before the plunge, a reef of wind
muscling under the wing and all sense
suspended for the span you inhabit

like the pure white interval over
the page before the broad sweep of ink
flows upwards and outwards as a rope

soars to coil in hieroglyph, closeknit.
We might have said that it's nothing
so simple, but a black and red, near extinct

bird tumbling through tattered skylines,
through lead and rough gilt cloud with
a cry something like fresh-chalked signs

on a blackboard and signifying
nothing but an off-the-cuff crib,
a quick volta and its own delight in

the twist of it, the flurry.
We might have elaborated, the way
I dreamed a whole allegory

of improvisation: an underground lake,
a newspaper cockle boat unassimilable
as similitude, black and white and red, its wake

unfurling like a dark stroke of ink
and in the prow like an unkempt raven
or chough, a black umbrella, unsettling,

snapping open and shut as if for take-off
like something we might have laughed at,
something you might have made a meaning of.

III

There are no likenesses here, there are only the mountains
behind the mountains, the lakes
the snowcap and the combed black peaks –
this summit is not a pyramid,
that ridge is not a fortification

though it looks like one.
Though this range with its improbable
enjambements springs to mind your line
breaks and their soaring double-jointed descent
down a sheer surface

it is not a poem.
The lake has a boat-station and a name,
a creek flows out of it to the north:
these are things to hold on to.
It has kayaks tossed on the wake of motorlaunches

in a push-me-pull-you cradling,
a stony cabal of water against the hull subdued
in the soundlock under the mountain.
Here, on the face of it, you could imagine a climber
solitary and wedged in the rock's lifelines

without likenesses, or a crevice,
a rope, a pass. You could imagine anything:
voices of the dead from Spirit Island,
the high articulated laughter of a loon.
Two moose swimming the lake left

to right and bobbing slightly –
not standing for anything, just getting across
the wake of the returning launch under
the clattering rise and fall, the uninterpretable toothcomb
notes of a jay.

Elegy
(for Giles)

In a room, in the circle of ash, charcoal:
your scuppered boots, half-attentive frown,
the television on. Fast at the corner of
your eyes, a long diagonal slide into
the ball, the astonishing pass, the remote
surge, shoulder-surfing noise.

In a line on your page on a train
are the children with impossibly large
sketchbooks skewed like kites in
a slipstream of hills going west
and over the page the hat-trick:
your smile balanced like an unfamiliar

beaver-skin. Or, going back a bit,
in viridian shade an open parasol,
trellises, terracotta urn, and the book
with its corner turned down at
the page where in pen and ink
your cat fits an edgy arm-chair

and around him are the fish-bone,
the wish-bone, the open cage –
things that stuck, these surroundings,
like the passenger's door-handle,
that sheepskin rug, and the way
you'd stride slantwise from car

to house, or pencil the scrollwork
of a cast-iron chair circuitous as
the cat's track record round the edge
of a field, so faint it's only the weaving
of the ears in grass that shows where
it passes into something else again.

Russian Dolls

So they arrived, and found the shape of things
was a pear tree, a run of red brick
garden walls like the anatomy of a lost
civilisation, and a black and white cat
balled against pink peonies.

So they bought paint and papers and made
the house an interior. They took things in.
Sun spotted the ripening pears.
The evenings stretched like an elegy.
And they looked down on the skeletal north-

north-westerly semaphore of aerials, grew
self-contained. In autumn, as the fruit fell,
they could feel it: a new core shouldering
into place like a gold pear hardening
under the motley pear's skin.

A Grip on Thin Air

(2000)

But of that supposicyon that callyd is arte,
Confuse distributyve, as Parrot hath devysed,
Let every man after his merit take his parte.

JOHN SKELTON
Speke Parrot

Migration

First, there was the waking,
each day, to a lightness
they couldn't place. The air
stretched tight as a sheet;
the sun on their whitewashed

walls was flexible, or at any rate
warm and rounded to the touch.
It clung about them; they moved
shadowless, footsteps dropping like
stones to the light-resounding bay.

Daily their home gathered weed,
names, string. Sea-changed,
their eyes lost transparency;
they saw the house as it was:
a wholly new thing.

When the dreams came:
tarred and feathered bundles
of prehistory, their webbed feet
clay. They came overnight,
silently, as homing birds

to their owners, whose waking
each day was to a clogged grey
dawn, whose night-time shadows
had wings, scything steeply
above their narrow beds.

Arrival

Still travelling, he dreams up his arrival –
lime-green and mottled. Grey. There will be
boats, increasingly; first, an interruption
of the sea's languid splay, the engine
hesitantly changing its beat. There's no quay
in sight yet, but in the waves' slap-and-lull

a distant hint of land: a quiet, elemental
preparation for change. Meantime, shapes loom
suddenly; as suddenly vanish, unidentified:
tawny for buoys, rust for a dredger? Few guide-
lines here for the homing ear and eye. A gloom
descends on the sundeck. This is an interval;

the slow outreach of the bay, the predictable
greying cliffs and greyish rain. Harold's tomb
lies to the north, with above it a rise of tide-
marked fields. This is watercolour country, wide
reaches of drab rippled by offshore sound: boom
of light-ships, a siren gull. Houses are vertical:

white pinions to the land's falling off – impersonal.
If a door opens, and someone calls soundlessly
across the street, the ship's beneath her observation.
Its passengers are daily and bear no relation
to her, to whom the three dimensions of the estuary
are home, and arrivals a fourth, unremarkable.

The Skater

Quick against the dead
of landscape, a fluster
of movement with at its edges
hesitancy.

There's a fresh element
this winter: the water's
new solidity, which draws
an expectant cluster

of spectators, and one
in black, who pulls away
without effort, his track
long and powdery

parallels, cross-hatching.
And quick – such surety
in motion it's a vanishing
trick of the light,

as against the sun
between shoulder-high banks
his figure dwindles
across a country that's dark

and barely charted but
by the skates' straight lines
of passage. A territory
where fish show amber in ice,

their eyes unblinking under
the imprint of skates and sky,
roundly containing them:
curved and in miniature.

Norfolk

Drive-through country, between
the last inland stop and a promise
of the sea. The sky brims
with its approaching victory;

fields are its undertow,
converged on the middle distance where
poplars flaunt the river's
absence or an oak avenue

too abruptly ends. Young
corn springs brash as pins in its furrows
and slowly an over-
lifesized scarecrow swings its shadow

over a gathering
of pigeons and roll-gait gulls. Its dull
creaking plumbs the sky, while
the two-tone whistle of passing

geese beats out the bounds of
the horizon and at the field's edge
the first train rackets by.
Mornings, the country is testing

its limits, but at dusk
the corn's a deep grey weight of shadow,
fields lying low beneath
dark and sentinel trees, waiting

for the night to draw in
like a sea-mist, undoing distance
and making of houses,
lighthouses over ebbing fields.

Where, lying awake, you
might almost hear the red-smocked scarecrow
shifting (each morning he's
slightly further off) and an owl

whose hunting call drifts long
and horizontally while houses
lie like echoes under
the vocal strata of the sky.

Emigrants

Will know where they are by the absence
of trees, of people – the absence
even of anything to do. All
luggage is in transit; nothing at all
to do but watch from the empty house

through the empty window. The sky
is underlit, and under the sky
a lake; pewter, reflecting. A road.
Yellow buses turn at the end of the road,
if it is an end. Reeds block the view.

This bus is wheel-deep in them; it swims
along the lake's edge and a swan swims
towards it. They pass. And here, at last,
are two people, waiting for the last
bus out, or just standing, as people must

stand here often, leaning on the wind,
deep in reeds, and speechless in the wind
as if *lake* and *sky* were foreign words
to them as well: standing without words
but without need of them, being at home.

Elemental

Lowlands. The air is liquid with rain
that doesn't fall; the sun hangs in suspension.
Light is seeping away down the track
that runs like a tightrope
from Krimpen to Ouderkerk, glistening
black between black, glistening, untranslatable
sloten (slots, cuts, or drainage ditches?

– they are not canals). Two cyclists pass.
The track hisses like a live wire; tyremarks crass
silver on black. The air's saturate.
With speed, colour bleeds from
their backs: swimming, scarlet, a comet's
tail. There are tidemarks strung out across the sky;
the water is rising. A heron hoists

itself, weightily, into thin air;
its counterpart goes down, an underwater
cloud blocking the underwater sun.
Land's down to a float-line
between two elements, is rarely
firm or *dry* (on a flood-tide, pavements ripple
in formation) except when, winters,
frost seals it in; skaters
take to the roads like water, cutting
across roof-tops, circling the upstairs windows
of houses grounded solidly on

their own reflections between paint-brush
poplars and crescented fish, over a pale
sun which marks time against the under-
side of the ice. The air's
so crackled with frost it seems it too
would bear and even the town's red-brick frontage
looks firm, like a destination.

But the thaw will begin at night on
the river high above town; it will come in
like an act of translation with wind
from the west in tidal
waves, sounding off roofs and ridge-tiles like
ships' wooden hulls, like ice floes overhead or
the full, reflected moon rebounding.

Beginning Her Journey

(after a wood-engraving by Anne Hayward)

The portents are mixed. She has achieved a corner seat
facing the engine, but by the sheer weight of it, the sun
must be setting. This means she is travelling east.

It is clearly winter. Outside the window, trees articulate
the air. The glass is thin: the long grasses seem almost
in the carriage, and branches teasle the gap between

the door and the door's reduced reflection on the far
side of the track. The cropped field is stubbly and plush as
the upholstery. She has a prickling in the back of the knees

and a basket, and a wary look. Her hair is cut precisely
as the grass, each fine white mark a defining act,
irrevocable: white on black. She is growing out of the dark.

The mahogany window-frames and square silvered latch
suggest that all this was some time ago: if the seats
were coloured, they would be green and blue. And nothing

has happened yet. The train could be anywhere; it makes
no difference to her. She has never heard the adage
if that's where you're going, I wouldn't start from here.

She carries herself like a chalice. Upright, a little tense,
even the hands folded in her lap are alert to catch
her basket, chance, the fluted air, and not to spill it.

Although this isn't quite the future it is still life.
She hasn't decided yet what line she will take on it,
but she looks so like herself that someone's sure to notice,

and when she arrives she will make a perfect picture in
her cobalt dress, stepping down from this east-bound train
or (if her seat faces backwards) from this train to the west.

Flight-path

Heathrow: on the map, it's enough to convince
the earth's flat as a springboard. The scarlet-edged
loops and loveknots of motorway, sliproad and fly-
over which promise all travellers (eventually)
a safe return, stumble on a runway: a loose end.

And though their steep trajectories imply
a fall, planes leave no less decisively now
than ships once went down, mercurial as fish
sky-hooked on some celestial line, each wake
a temporary gothic arc, a cartographer's pen

flourishing into the third dimension and proving
there are countries there, if only we could find them,
above the cumulus, under the light which scales
the plane's sides. Which is pure fabrication.
But new arrivals have horizons behind the eyes.

This is not, they say, *their intended destination*,
clutching about them their baggage like bedding,
their four-fold carriers, fishing-line, and the faded
black straw hat which in between-time over
the Atlantic with the sky singing like siren song

that here, but for gravity, even home might be
a place of choosing, was big enough to drown
the world in.
                    Looking down on the lights of London
settling like coins in an inverted hat's crown,
their sights are setting. They are descending (coats

trailed awkwardly as damaged wings) heavy-footed
through the great glass hall, cake-walking down
escalators and along corridors; scaling the rack
of the multi-storey in staggered and limited ascent.
They are grounded on the sliproad; they are slowly

dispersing, while overhead between planes, a long v
of Canada geese buffets in to land across the motorway,
a formation of gulls swivels like a strobe, and a glider circles,
trailing string. No one watches. They are expected;
they have arrived. At best, this is a point of departure.

Women and Secrets

(after Tirzah Ravilious)

It is the shock of absence
on waking: that shaking certainty
I heard nothing. By night, the over-
familiarity of the room oppresses: clenched
sheet, open door, and the precise proximity
of a husband's back. It was all a cover-

up: it was nothing – nothing to be spoken
of, nothing to disturb. But there are two ways
of telling. (The woman sits upright; eyes
riddle the dark.) There's a story in broken
nights, an interlude, quieter than the days'
pastiche, and more private. The simple ties

– wife, artist, mother – fall away. (Draw
the covers closer.) There's time for exploration:
motives past and present (crossed in love? a yen
for solitude?). But there's also this: not raw
psychology, but *I heard nothing.* No explanation,
but the upright jolt of waking. And then?

Perfect Pitch

Why, you've got a grip on thin air
as if it were a punt pole or a bike's
palmed accelerator, as if you could wrest
the perfect word from it, honing it down

to the marrow. You've really put your back
into this argument, and when you let rip,
yes, these are the bare bones of the case:
I'd take a punt with you out to the Marston

Ferry, dance all night and ride pillion
to Brighton with the wind cutting away
from our feet like ice. I'd cross swords.
I'd learn to fence. But above all, when you

pause and spread your hands, letting fly
a catchword with a wicked spin, I want
to give chase: I want to pick up the ball
and run with it. If this is a duel, I want to win.

It is high summer. Outside, trees are poised
on their shadows as on pedestals.
A boy circles the lawn, letting drift
a frisbee languidly from the quick-quick-

slow unhinging of his arm: a yellow disc
snickering the heat-haze. (The sky is keyed up
to a ridiculous pitch.) And fluently, as if
cutting across a line of argument or mirror

image, a second boy intercepts. Here it comes
again, almost silently. The first man feigns
a miss. One slip of the wrist and it's upon us –
preposterous, flightless, plastic fledgling

in the lecture room; cascades of glass,
torrents of abuse. And we could pick it up
and run with it (*a divine visitation, a bolt
from the blue*), and I could tell you then –

It is your turn. You hesitate. (This is a difficult
point to put across.) But now you are winging it:
the word immaculate, refined. You smile. You've
the sky in your eyes. The glass is already singing.

Landscape

Picture it like this: a length
of beach, and two people,
monochrome,
passing down the long, horizontal
reach of sea, and shadow, and sky.
How the eye
homes (almost absently) to these, figures
in landscape: the slow

movement, the caricature lilt
and drag of shadows on
sand, angled
as the hollows and rounds of speech. Love?
is its question, a hesitant
lift, quiet
as waking. The two shadows gesture, dove-
tail; words test the air

as a sleeper tries the morning
with silhouetted hand:
will it bear?
Light pours across their long silence, then
flares: the answer rises steady
as a kite,
absurd in its trust that two sticks and tissue
skin will make a bird,

flesh out the sky a little. Love:
at least half imaginative,
a question
even in reply. The two figures
edge across the beach, shadowing
new ground in
a silence which draws parallels as charged
and telling as speech.

Likeness

And if I said I saw it like this – the cut and dash
of your hands and coat-tails a marginal gloss:
the flick of the cuff and elongated index indicating
Nota, mark this well, like the showman's patter,
the smooth consecutive doodles on the surface
of the Cherwell up by the rollers before it slides
into the weir which are like so many flourishes
with silk handkerchiefs to take us all unsuspecting
up to the edge (if I said: in telling, you'd make this
sound like Niagara), these would be likenesses
as light under the bridge by the millpond takes the shape
of the wind like leaves and the volume of dark below it's
like a solid – if it weren't for that fish bowing it distractedly
and never next where it's expected, but the way pennies
dropped in a plastic washing-up bowl at a fête cut off,
glinting, at an angle, so it goes oblique, darkling from shadow
to shadow like groundswell, like the slow movement
under the surface rapids and razzmatazz of the weir. And yes,
I'd say we were both like that, and set and matched in it like
a balancing act, and always testing the water: so that if I
asked you round I'd half expect you to show with a parrot
(like out on a rope over Niagara you need a punt pole
and a scarlet silk neck-tie for distraction), and though
I've never yet found you juggling apples in Tesco I guess
if I tossed you one in passing you'd catch and flip it back
pat, like a likeness, as if you didn't even need to think.

Polyptych: Annunciation

I *The Art-Critic*

I wasn't noticing especially. My eyes were dazzled.
It was hot outside, and the sun was feathered
through the lights like an arrow-shaft. I must
have looked right through them. I was thinking
about the view: a clutch of bicyclists like rooks
on the tow-path, pointers of poplar out on
the horizon, a swift flicker of wings and the river
running like an uninterrupted conversation.
Closer to, an angel with a copper trumpet. I wasn't
looking at the staircase, or the people on it:
if anything, I noticed the man in a stove-pipe hat
(in the heat that day) standing by a window
in the reading room, a far-away noise like scaffolding
or a metal punt pole mishandled, and later,
when I went out, the porter sweeping up feathers,
telling me the library doesn't keep a cat.

II *The Angel*

They say this takes practice, but refuse to let us know,
till the last minute, who'll be sent for the next rehearsal:
we set off all unprepared as the Christmas Eve soloist
at King's, mouth rounded in parody of that opening *o*.
He at least has the advantage of knowing the words.
We plummet blind, like justice or liberty, coming up
below the skin of some unsuspecting mortal as if in
a diving-bell, adjusting ourselves to the cut of his spine,
the set of his eyes, and shyly glancing out at the world.
We're never told, beforehand, who it is we're looking for.
It's that, and the wings, that cause most difficulty:
we leave them off, of course, but there's no hiding
the habit of wearing them: we arch our shoulders
and stride out fast as if every other step were the point
of take-off, and our parted lips declare we are always
just about to tell... People stare. At first, though,
that day, it all seemed easy. I arrived and settled in:
not Cambridge, in fact, but the other place: the Bodleian.

A good broad stair to pace on and look out for her.
I thought the flower should be a metaphor. And then
she called me. Perhaps I was wrong – but I was sure.
And so I smiled her full in the face, and handed it over:
the seed of imagination, luminous and ready to deploy
itself between the first and second ventricle of the brain,
the stamen and filament split into the feathered warp
and weft of the double wings of a crocus vivisected
on a lightbox, roots fibrous and tentative as angel-hair.
As tow. She took it very well, I remember thinking.
She smiled straight back at me. And I fell.

III *Mary*

Of course I recognised him at once. I'd seen him before,
that boy: Renaissance man, works on the quattrocento.
Sits in the short arm of the reading room. As to why
I called him back, I'm not quite sure. He was going fast.
There was a disturbance vapoured in the air around him;
he seemed to be carrying – could they have been iris? –
and I thought he'd dropped something, so I said 'Stop –
you've forgotten your...' '...lines?' I think he asked,
but he hadn't. Not for a minute. And I couldn't say
I wasn't expecting it. I'd been distracted all summer,
feeling my eye slip down the white channel between text
proper and marginal gloss: losing my grip. Outside
they were ringing down the scaffolding round Duke Humfrey
like a discord of outsize wind-chimes and there was a sense
of something permanently on the brink of happening
somewhere else, as when on *Morse* the choir sings *Gloria
Gloria* and corpses tumble behind the scenes. That day
in particular it was far too hot. The girl on the next desk
was strumming *Bohemian Rhapsody* under her breath;
there was a man with a pickaxe out by the sign which says
Silence Please. This is a Library; the room was humming
like a tuning-fork and the light was out of its element.
I went for a drink. He was tall in the angle of the stairs,
and I was glad, I think. All the same, afterwards at my desk,
I wondered '...so here I am, happily settled, I'd have said,
and trying to turn myself into an academic, and you come
and tell me *this*?' And what exactly? To recapitulate:
'I've forgotten my diary; I'll send you an e-mail. Perhaps

we could make a date?' And I can no more pluck the sense
from it than trace the shot of lead in the soft sift of feather-
down that's become of my heart and head, or spell my name
with this lightweight excuse of a pen I'm landed with,
which for all its strong primary bent like his silhouette
about the shoulders and its gold tip is – indubitably – a quill.

IV *Mary and the Angel*

It's no secret that God's in the details –
it's a commonplace. So when the angel
descends again, this time (a Tuesday)
in the upper reading room, it's no surprise
we concentrate on the neat brown spines
of Early English Texts or the man over by
the window in a hat like Arnolfini's
and draw the whole annunciation
irrevocably into the present tense.

So is it strange I can't always remember
your face, or only in time and place specific
locations? I've your smile at Worcester,
your chin up St Giles and cheekbones
by the faculty. But your eyes are different:
the way they throw light like darts, like a leap
of faith or the mercury twist of water tossed
from a glass, how could I possibly forget?
And I'm not sure what this amounts to, yet –

but when you swing the corner fast as a pole-
vaulter over the edge of a precipice, the ceiling
chinks like a lid under pressure and if you stop
to say *Lunch?* I'd call this room the spinning
centre of the flat earth as the roof goes up
and the scaffolding comes down in a chorus
of halleluiahs – and then you've gone.
And your face? No. Even looking I've lost it.
It's a question of focus. It's your eyes in a storm.

V *The Porter*

I can tell them at once. They're the ones whose smile
rings out like the sun cracked from a weather-vane
and whose eyes have everything to declare.
And when I search their bags – sure, they have
books, like the others, but in among the detritus
of pencils, paperclips and pens there'll be some
small thing they simply can't account for – a broken
feather, pressed crocus petal or a dusting of torn
gold-leaf. And I'll know to expect another set, come
evening, cut with the same gravity as a gown
but softer to the touch: all filaments of gossamer
silk, and swansdown. About the structure I'm less sure:
buckram, perhaps, or whalebone? I've never dissected
a pair, though we know as we take them in to lost
property it means another one's cut loose out there:
has hung up his wings for surplus, and won't be back soon.

Equivocation

After all this time I presume when we meet
face to face we will be like two apprentices
pitting themselves against the sheer weight
of a sheet of glass, the learning curve of the arms
at full stretch like an illusionist's handkerchief
before the penny drops, white-knuckled, breath
against misted breath as we try to take the measure
of this thing between us with the same shaky
precision as when you pour wine, I touch the stem
of the glass, and we glance apart: wrong-footed,
laughing, apprehensive to the fingertips. *Impasse.*

So – it's time we carried it off: tip-toe fingered,
and cheek to cheek as in a waltz while over
our heads a number ten bus goes up
like a balloon, a zebra entwines two belisha
beacons and the sky sheers off like a velux –
there's a risk, of course, but it's nothing much
to gaping across an empty space, aghast less
at the crash than the aftermath: the slack sky,
the pedestrian paces of the street stony as
denial, and flirting off round the corner of the eye,
a red rag that marks the end of a glazier's van.

Bilingual

New weight of language on the tongue;
the tongue tied: intractable, dumb.
The mouth takes shape in a new medium.
Its own breath is less than malleable.
                    Speech becomes sculpture:
a six-month-slow baroque contortion
to form one sentence:

ik stond met m'n mond vol tanden

Sounds freshly unearthed; the mouth
furred, lichen-locked; the tongue's tip curled.
Translation's a technicality: muscular
mastery of the letter R; long division
of the plaintive seagull syllables *ee, ui, ij:*

een enkele reis, alstublieft

The first words are rotund: pristine,
hard-pressed pebbles on the tongue.
Until the moment of revelation
when they burst like grapes against
the palate, and the tongue, unleashed,
unfurls like a cat and cries: *I am loose
(los). Undone. Just look. I am translated.*

Because words are not things

In the portakabin (classroom) the master is dictating.
Words swell from deep in his stomach: purple,
tawny, and umber. They rumble about the room
like thunderclouds. The children take them down
as if they were flesh and blood words.
As if they were flesh and blood children.
There are red clouds tumbling over my head.
I look down at my neat red fountain pen.
Then: WHAM. PAF. A thick black comic strip
punchline between the eyes. A thunder-clap.
This is a word I recognise. *Komkommertje.*
I write it down. It means a small cucumber.
It doesn't sound much like a small cucumber
but like the body-language of other girls
in the playground. Clapping. Playing tag
in tidy square-toed shoes with bright
square-cut hair flapping like rags out to dry.
Kom-kom-kommertje. My hair is plaited and dull.

I look out of the window and there is a bull
in the playground. I want to say: *look, there is
a bull out in the playground*, but I don't know
the words for playground or for bull.
The bull snorts and paws the ground like a bull
in picture-books. Red smoke spurts from his nostrils
in two small thunder-clouds. He is going to charge.
I think he will charge first through the empty hall
and into the paint-store and that he'll toss his huge
head around between the shelves and PAF WHAM
his horns will prang the squishy tubes of paint
and WHAM SPLAT he will break down the door
and charge into the classroom with glutinous scarlet
and mauve and midnight blue poster paint clogging
his horns. He will stamp the floor so the classroom
(portakabin) rattles and because I don't know the words
for *scream* or *shout* or *run*, I shall have to defend
myself silently. I shall throw down my pen.

Lost and Found

On Wednesday last, in the vicinity
of the Kingston Road: item: one voice,
exact tenor and timbre unknown
but believed to be romantic (perhaps
something of a drifter). Frequently
sighted in the past by overnight travellers
on trains and coaches, in open-mouthed,
incessant, disembodied discourse
on the far side of the glass.
Believed to be making for the coast.
(Boat-owners please check your sheds.)

Its hideouts are various and it's rarely
in the same place twice but you'd know
it if you found it. It might be in the silence
when a crow stoops in a scything
graceline to pluck a leaf from the beak
of its own, moated reflection; it might be
floundering in the song sung by someone
rained on at a bus-stop, and although
you can't tell it by its gait or what it wears,
you will know it by the sense of suddenly,
incredibly, believing your own ears.

The Master-Builder

Not the birds of the air show such determination:
such a gathering of wood gathering dust gathering
good intentions. Plucked from skips, from hedges,

and the renovation of the local pub, to shape
a ramshackle wigwam in the living-room:
like jackstraws, like a life-sized game of spillikins.

Let these be the foundations, the work of the busy
right hand. Already, it has made out an architrave
and a piece of skirting. It clatters about its duty.

It is sensible. It has things to do in the kitchen.
While upstairs (six planks and a length of string)
the left hand moves mountains with a pencil.

The right hand clutches a screwdriver; the left hand
holds the house in a nutshell.
                                        Love, it says,
I have whittled you an oasis from this empty skin,

from these base red bricks and black misfirings.
The bedroom and bathroom are nave and chancel.
There will be a lightwell over the stairs where

light falls light-fingered through the chestnut tree.
The walls will be a garden, and the garden
a tapestry. We'll plant quince, crab and maple:

I've planned it to the circumference of the ripple
from the fountain.
                        In the kitchen, the right hand
extends its sore black thumb. The left hand is a poet.

The right hand has put its head in the oven.
Left hand, right hand, there is no communication.
Between them, rain moulds the bedroom ceiling

with mountain ranges splaying into tracery like leaves.
Between them, the kitchen sink has come adrift;
the house rests uneasily as a fledgling.

Both hands make shift; they take long views of things.
At night, the house lights up like a habitation.
Through the uncurtained windows there are signs

of life: a toaster, a red rose, and in every room
the intricate weft of wood that at first glance looks
something like a cross between a life-raft and an icon.

House

(after Rachel Whiteread)

Object lesson. Its walls are
Braille-blind: smooth sides of concrete in place
of windows pressed flat
as the palms of a child who wants out,
wants the collie running in the park, the long
green belt of the park itself,
the street-lights, all-night

petrol and trains that rattle-
snake the viaduct for Harwich, for
Liverpool Street. Want's
simple: *I live here. This is my home.*
A blue plaque marks the fall of the first doodle-
bug; abruptly end-terraced
number forty-six

is in scaffolding again
fifty years on, doors stuck in their jambs,
shadows sifting side-
ways with a sandtimer tilt behind
blinds. Up the road number 193 is railed:
opaque as a monument,
looking-glass chimney

breasts too straight-forward for words.
(*What for? – Why not?*) Even the trace-marks
of the stairs are one-
dimensional as an unravelled
palimpsest. It's as if memory could be
cast whole, and a house reduced
to its logical

elements, as if it weren't
more: the fierce and fragile habit of
belonging, footsteps
persisting in their pattern even
under scaffolding, slipping as fluently
as any cat or burglar
through blocked doors, over

the invisible paper
roses on the walls, and up and out
through the skylight. Filled
and sealed: an absence so tangible
it is itself a kind of hoarding; the park
no park but *the view*
from here, even as

ball and chain weigh slowly in,
the suddenly empty air runs rings
round the child calling
his dog and the grass stretches without
interruption to the railway and
the dark, marginal doodle
that is the canal.

Travelling Light

Like flotsam curtseying on the spot, things
are coming back to him. Honeysuckle. Lavender.
The weighty press and scent of blackcurrant
bushes as he walked out, and his mind edgy

as a cat testing the sun, all vertebrae.
A five-runged swimming-pool ladder hung
from a brick garden wall, but no pool.
How this (more than anything) irked him.

And the way the village High Street dead-ended
in *Danger Cliff Fall Road and Path Destroyed*
and someone had raised the red and white
barrier to an arch, and someone was growing roses.

How the last house that day was aerial –
yellow tin butterfly roof open to the sky,
marram grass coiled in chicken wire and a wall
of railway sleepers topped with blue and green

bottles like skittles, like a seismograph – and how
the breakwater below crissed and double-crossed
before coming up with a red flag with an air of
surprised finality. Why he took it for an omen,

so when the plane strummed over and its propeller
cut a corkscrew spiral like the final flourish in
a game of consequences or conclusive proof
that air is thicker than water he looked askance

at the barricade and for *Danger* read *Dance*
and brushed past the roses to step out in
its wake lightly as a cat with artful insouciance
ringing down the ladder onto the lawn.

Skelton at Diss

As for what they dredged from the mere
two days ago: of that, as of many things,
he will remain silent. Neither fish,
fowl, nor good red herring, but fleshly
proof the old Scots allegation is true:
Englishmen have tails. As for Christian
burial, he will leave that to the sexton.

It has grown difficult even to pray.
In nomine patri – but the wind is incarnate:
it is inside his head and torments there
like a caged bird. He can sense
the shape of it: walks his own mind
gingerly, not to startle it, as daily
he must edge around the mere.

He knows now: there was no miracle.
When Christ walked on water it was
purely practical. There's no going straight
anywhere round here, but always instead
a soughing over-shoes in mud with only
the wind for support. It rings hollow.
A slipper hold the tail is of an eel.

It's not the edginess that bothers him.
He has been to Yarmouth and seen
the sky tethered off behind the horizon
like a loose canvas flap. He has seen
the herring-catch brought in and thought
that words used to be like that:
illumined silver, quick-still, runnel-backed

and in profusion, which now are sparse,
wind-whittled: brittle dead wood. He talked
to fishermen about tides and erosion,
and saw that to write again, would mean
to write in short sentences. The tongue
a pillar of salt, the self a walking contradiction:
breathless, and laureate. He returned to Diss.

The wind cut and thrust like a courtier;
the sky settled like a weight on his back.
And it was then he found them,
his congregation, hummocked round
the mere like fallen angels, and they glummed
on him and parted ranks to show him
their catch. He heard himself pray

with words that came straight from the tongue
though his mind disremembered them
and in insistent non-sequitur pictured how
only the day before, some hunting parson's
hawk had stooped and left by the west door
a clutch of grey tail feathers and the single
immaculately shorn-off wing of a pigeon.

From Barbara Hepworth's Garden

This photograph was taken through the eye
of the sculpture, where water lies cupped
like a fleck of light on the retina, reflecting
the bronze which reflects elements of the sky.

The eye fragments. Beyond it are pieces of visitors
to the garden: half a body, an uncapped head,
an arm. They are hard to follow. The eye
gives a restricted view. (From the street below

the garden itself is invisible.) Lying back
in a black and white shell of a chair in
the conservatory – just out of the picture –
a voice circles phrases, lazily, like smoke rings,

like paper birds. The visitors are passing (one
with an orange rucksack). They are standing up,
they are moving away from the edge of this snap-
shot they have no part in. The voices continue.

There is no interruption.

The town is staggering up the hill. The people
are climbing up the town. They are flying kites
from the burial mounds on Trencrom.
Children run rings round the Men-an-Tol.

On the south coast above Newlyn bay, all
the maidens have turned to stone, *the earth
rising and becoming human.* The sea grinds
sand for its shores; the land is its own elegy.

(There is no interruption.)

Moving upwards and inland, away from the kites
and the sea, the voices grow dissonant.
The garden is fading in the sun. Its shadows
are monolithic: like stone, colouring differently

under different carvers' hands. And this is the art
not the photograph of memory: the need to rebuild,
repeatedly, the smile on the living face, to cradle it
like china, looking *not back in time, but through it*

like water: in the hand, a snapshot, in the workshop
a sculpture wanting form. There is life in it. It will
cut to the quick. The form is pierced. The eye is full
of water. Reflections rain from the sky like hammer-blows:

solidly, and without interruption.

Shelf-life

These are the parings of a life, the incidentals
Which flake away as a potter parts dry
Waste clay from her pot.
        Leaving bare essentials:
Kiss and kick of shoe on a spinning disc,
Sunlight cobwebbed, sagging across the shed.
The potter says it's a question of centring.
Her leg swings from the knee, her wheel spins
Like the flat earth on its invisible axis:
She throws clay plumb as the first stone
Or a brilliant guess. Lifeless, it spins.
        She cups her hands, pools
The cool, revolutionary weight of it.
It evolves expansively. Elastically. Spinning.
Bulk in indigo shade; highlight tipped.
        The room is very quiet.
Her hands take the pot's runnelled imprint
        Containing, self-contained
She stoops, considers.
        Yes, provisionally
The pot is done.
        The wheel slows.
The room settles like dust in the sun.

Life-writing

It is a matter of questioning. The bare essentials:
Hieroglyph. Photograph. Reportage. Memory.
At twelve she climbed trees.
        Her hands were ringed
In earth, clay, diamond, emerald, or opal.
She had a husband and two sons.
She had two gardens, she loved travel.
Auburn-haired, she'd have liked to wear orange.
She'd tumble downhill to save her hat from a pond.
A clutch of facts: *obiter*, incidental.
Beneath, there's a shelf-life shaping:
A shadow-self. Space at the centre of a ring.
Under cupboards, lost thread spins its colours
In darkness; in darkness glasses lustre to themselves.
        And the moral is –
Unfathomable. This is not a story;
It's a balance of probabilities and plans.
        Turn her mugs in the sun:
Revolutionary, ringed, it's as close as she'll come.
        This is a kind of equilibrium:
Absence contained. The laying on of hands.
The light grows fractious as mosaic.
There is work in progress. It is provisional.

(for Jessica Lilian Griffiths, née Broad, 1909–1987)

Speech
(for R.E.G., 1910-1991)

Long periods, these. The voice rises,
falls down a century, careful
in its questions of time, and spacing.
His hands set the pace, tracing
lines of thought, cradling his subject
like string. Lights

and shadows, these movements of a voice,
balancing the black, the off-white.
He lets them sink to conclusion. Hands
lie pooled in the shade of his lap;
the diver in its glass bottle dips:
a bright slip-

stream in the water's darkness. He angles
with the straight pins of speech, bent on
a needle-point of light in the mind's
opaque eye. His hands lift, the palms
open. The diver plumbs glassy depths.
Bubbles rise

like questions, open endings of thought,
but a sentence falls, bottoms out.
Watch through the glass: it is a sharp-edged
penny that cuts through water lightly as
through the conjuring hand, coin on coin
till towers

rise between his fingers. He plies them
round a small space of air, his voice
shaping true, and false, as he pays out
his conjectures. There is a pause.
Then the answer forms. The diver bobs,
and rises.

The Art of Memory

First, you must choose a system, any system.
Think of a wall. Divide it
(like the backdrop of an early theatre)
into five parts: the first tall and thin,
the others, square. Now, fix each with
an image, any image.
Traditionally a ship
and obelisk would appear, but if you'd prefer
choose a spinning-top, take a goldfish.

Next, select those things you want to remember:
a small glass fox, Blackfriars Bridge
(early morning, with sunlight scything off
the dome of St Paul's), a pub garden
embrace. Lift them, carefully, one
by one, and pin each of them
to a memory-place, as
a child blindfold at a party pins the donkey's
tail. Stand back; watch patterns develop.

The method's never been known to fail. Look. Here
is the bridge. Rehearse it; walk
round it; walk underneath, along the sleek
purling muscle of the river,
along the belly-side of things. Snake-
skin dapplings reflect and warp
the riveted steel girders
which support dry land's smooth progression over
mooring posts, over acanthus leaves

flourishing on the capitals of phalanxed
Corinthian columns gone
astray (the piers for an absent railway,
mammoths shouldering thin air). Note that
the view from the bridge overleaps them.
Then move on. Here's the house where
Wren watched St Paul's grow buoyant
in the first floor drawing-room window, and below
in the garden is a pool heavy

with goldfish, and apple trees in silhouette
overlaid on the clean cut,
obeliskesque powerstation's profile,
over the precise, diamond-hinged
geometries of cranes lifting thatch
for the great Globe's rebuilding
(Bankside and Rose Alley grown
ankle-deep in reed), lifting time hesitantly,
swinging, reversing the pendulum

weighted by a clutch of straws, and containing,
roofing in the tiring-house
wall. Architecting time. (Downstream under
the river on a long red carpet
Brunel raises a glass: *to progress*,
and twelve dozen reflected
candle-flames wrap themselves round
the bowl.) And all the while the people are passing:
awkward, unfathomable, moving

people, with briefcases, bags, or three balls of
string. Behind them is St Paul's.
They flicker past the balustrade like gold-
fish in the sun; they pause in the bays
to exchange views. Doors open and shut.
The river cuts and shuffles
light, the spoken words eddy:
freighted, evanescent, impassable. Cross-
currents, consequences, will run and run.

Abstract

I

He must have painted it that first
day abroad: white square
on a white background, the sun
rising solidly
against his bedroom wall. White noise:
an early train syphoning

over the viaduct, and five
clean syllables as
a man calls his dog. The sun
on the balcony
is almost audible; below,
the city is abroad, is

uncontainable. The window
flows over with it.
Say it's six a.m., and light.
The paving stones are too small;
the narrow houses
are straight up and down, all surface
without shadow. The windows

are curtained white. Say it's abroad.
It must reduce to
a question of texture, eye-
catching and abstract,
white square against a white background
on a white gallery wall.

II

The gallery itself would make
a composition:
on the right, an imbalance
of white squares and just
off-centre a dark dividing
line, its exterior glass

wall that's a formal point of rest.
Outside, the may swings
like a reflection; blackbirds
chatter in some high-
pitched tongue. The stream flings up broken
squares of light. On its bare

mesh, the painting's square-tipped brushstrokes
compose, optically,
a kind of disillusion.
The square in its two
dimensions is more solid than
the canvas which supports it,

more solid than the outside wall.
It's a breathing-space,
the artist at rest.
It's the cage which sings
and not the bird; it's sunlight on
his walls that first day abroad.

Parallel Motion

In the front room of the fourth-floor apartment
overlooking the harbour, a clock slowly pays out
one thin gold chain; slowly retracts the other

like a spider drawing float-lines back into its belly.
It is all face and no body: it hardly looks serious enough
to keep time. All doors in the flat have frosted glass

panels; the clock goes naked. At night its round white
moonface catches the lights from across the harbour;
looking back from Lion Bridge, each uncurtained window

holds an identical white dimple above the almost perpetual,
almost silent movement of the chains. On each floor
a clock modestly goes through the motions of gravity.

Behind the scenes, lifts rise with becoming gravity
on pulleys housed between the walls of the fourth floor.
Each night the apartment thrums with perpetual

motion. Wheels turn within walls, and each window
reflects the contained electric storm that is the harbour:
water rolling darkly as thunder with shimmering white

inverted highlights of neon; rain falling like glass,
the windows dazzled with rain. There is water enough:
the river pulses through town like a snake on its belly

between embankments, bearing tugs, barges, and all its other
traffic high above the houses. The lift hits sea-level about
the first floor. The clock hangs like a bubble in the apartment.

A poem against the kind of occasional verse

which starts with a long quavering line like the run-up
to a marginal doodle on a set of lecture notes, the sort
which starts as a circle, becomes an eye, grows a quiff
and some flowers which sprout from an enormous ear
that's attached to a retrospective tea-pot spout
and culminates in a set of legs like those which belong
to an occasional table of the unassuming kind which
can always be pushed (almost) to one side: not just because
it's a way of running a paperchase single-handed so even
the element of surprise is lost or because the ends of lines loiter
without intent like drunks on the pavement at closing-time but
mainly because of the pretence that the writer is simply
part of the scenery, part of a bar-stool or a swift triangle
of red skirt round the ellipse of the Sheldonian who has stumbled
upon herself as upon the occasional table or chair leg
and observed herself and written her down, unassuming
and pi as the artless voice on the telephone whispering
it's only me when really *it is I* all the time.

Errata

Page 1, line 8, for incorrigible read unredeemable
Page 5, line 9, for undeniable read indelible
Page 6, line 15, for unreliable read untellable

Dark, and the lights are out in all the houses.
The one streetlamp is swamped in sycamore,
all the hill's houses are cradled in root.
Leaves' shadow-selves crowd the walls like ivy.
The dark is laying it on thick, tonight.

Page 16, line 5, for untellable read unspeakable

The cat by the cellar window is a cat-shaped
absence, in black. The cellar window's a strip-light
at its feet, a chink: the earth opening up.
The air is sticky as ink.

Page 20, line 10, for supplicate read deny
Page 20, line 12, for deny read supplicate

Suppose the man in the cellar looked up,
he'd only see dark behind the darker spikes
of lavender and rosemary. (The cat is quite invisible.)
And he doesn't look up. He is exchanging words
painstakingly. Dust and ink lodge indelibly
in his thumb; it ghosts to its negative, a thumbprint.
He will leave his mark. He works in the half-dark
almost all night. Letter by letter, he is setting things right.

Page 22, line 3, for unspeakable read unjustifiable

He is locking up, he is getting a grip on this story
(the press with its oil-black rollers is waiting),
taking the lead weight of it between two hands,
tilting its lead-black against the ink-black
of the window; taking the first, fresh, impression.

Page 38, line 4, for simulate read assimilate
Page 40, line 2, for clarify read uncurtain

The first principle of design is leaving things out,
is in the spacing and the margins. Seven years
is the time-span for a complete change of skin.

Page 53, line 9, for past read future
Page 54, line 5, for amend read alter
Page 58, line 2, for alter read correct
Page 61, line 6, for correct read impose

The lines are unjustified. The errors are spawning.

Page 61, line 8, for impose read query
Page 62, line 5, the bracket should be closed
after the evidence, not after as clearly.

The chase frames the story.
Time and place are composed.

In the room above, a cat tests the floorboards.
It is six o'clock. It is almost morning.
Street-lights turn yellow; the sky comes adrift.
Clouds scud loose and dirt as newsprint.
The house will wake soon. Soon things will happen:
words will be exchanged: irrevocable, unredeemable,
demanding another night's work, and another, over-writing.

Page 70, line 2 for unjustifiable read unrevisable

There are not enough spaces between the days.

The Biographies of Poets

As always, it's a question of beginnings.
Born. In Letchworth, in Darlington. In nineteen
forty-two, or nineteen sixty-nine. Educated.
Attempts to educate were made. Initially
wrote, took up the pen, was published
in a large number of small magazines:
as always, acknowledgements are due

to the following and to the photographer
for the cropped chiaroscuro mug-shot
which you, the reader, scan for clues
or revelations beyond the black and white
lines, the changing dedications. Currently
(always) lives with husband, cat or lover.
Gardens, drinks, teaches: divides time.

Since the birth of their first child, runs
cooks swims; has taken to seeing things
between the cracks in the ceiling.
Whether in London Wales or Devon, wakes
daily, wearing the body as crumpled
linen, brimming with words like spirit,
like wine. Preserves, pickles, divides time

like water, senses its parting, currently,
into live wires, barley-twist columns, scales
of light: conceives vocab in response.
Since divorce paints skates jogs, collects
egg-cups, writes biographies (inverted
prisms). Luciferous, and flowing over with life
like water, like salt, sand, or wine.